From Ap... Expert

A civil engineer's memoir

To John & Valeria

with best wishes

Hugh

HUGH ALLAN

Published by Bakersboy Books

A CIP catalogue record for this book is available from the British Library.

ISBN 978-1-9996897-0-4

Book layout and cover design by Clare Brayshaw

Prepared and printed by:

York Publishing Services Ltd
64 Hallfield Road
Layerthorpe
York YO31 7ZQ

Tel: 01904 431213

Website: www.yps-publishing.co.uk

For Niall Alexander Ross Allan

Contents

Abbreviations

ACE	Association of Consulting Engineers
BA	British Airways
BSB	Baghdad Sewerage Board
BTEC	Business and Technology Education Council
CAD	computer aided design / drawing
CBI	Carl Bro International
CFCU	Central Finance and Contracts Unit (Romania)
CIWEM	Chartered Institution of Water and Environmental Management
DAB	Disputes Adjudication Board
DWAF	Department of Water Affairs and Forestry (South Africa)
EBRD	European Bank for Reconstruction and Development
EC	European Commission
EDEYA	Association of Greek Municipal Water Enterprises
EEC	European Economic Community
EPAL	Empresa Portuguesa das Águas Livres
EU	European Union
EYDE	Department of Greek Ministry of Public Works
FIDIC	International Federation of Consulting Engineers*
GOPP	Goal Orientated Project Planning
ICA	Instrumentation, Control and Automation
ICE	Institution of Civil Engineers
IDF	Israeli Defence Force

* Established as Fédération Internationale des Ingénieurs Conseils

ISPA	Instrument for Structural Policies for Pre-Accession (EC)
IWRM	Integrated Water Resource Management
JHH	John H Haiste
JV	Joint Venture
km	kilometre
LFA	Logical Framework Analysis
LGCSB	Local Government Computer Services Board (Ireland)
LNEC	Laboratório Nacional de Engenharia Civil (Portugal)
LTI	Lagoon Technology International
m	metre
M&E	mechanical and electrical
MEA	Middle East Airlines
NTU	National Technical University (Greece)
ONAS	Office National de l'Assainissement (Tunisia)
PASOK	Pan Hellenic Socialist Movement (Greece)
PRAG	Practical Guide to Contract Procedures for EC External Actions
QS	Quantity Surveyor
RCST	Royal College of Science and Technology
RE	Resident Engineer
RICS	Royal Institute of Chartered Surveyors
SCADA	Supervisory Control And Data Acquisition
SNP	Scottish National Party
SOWASP	State Organisation for Water and Sewerage Projects (Iraq)
TAE	The Academy of Experts
UN	United Nations
UNRWA	United Nations Relief Works Agency

Preface

I had been working on a project in Greece at the time. Reading my *New Civil Engineer,* the weekly house magazine of the Institution of Civil Engineers (ICE), I came across a review of an autobiographical book, written by a Jack Moore[1]. I cut the piece out from the magazine's page and put it into a 'to do' bundle of miscellaneous references that it was my habit to accumulate, in untidy fashion. Twenty years or so later, by that time having concluded the last of several projects in that country, I came across the tiny clipping in an office tidy up, sepia tinted with age. I sourced a copy of the book and read how, as a young civil engineer in the 1930s, Moore had given up his steady but rather uninspiring job in one of the big national firms of consulting engineers, where he was a bit of a cog in the wheel of that large organisation, to work up country in some fairly remote areas of Greece.

His tales struck a chord with me. During my years working there in the 1980s and 1990s I had visited some of the places where he had been posted, and there was a tenuous connection to one of the Greek partner firms with which my employer for thirty years had collaborated. A British construction company working in Greece was a bit of a rarity too in my experience, and to discover that Moore's employer was Henry Boot of Sheffield, the builder of the house in which I had lived for the first twenty five years of my life, was a pleasing coincidence.

After military service during WWII and employment locations in other locations post-war, Moore retired. Forty years on he returned to Greece to meet up with former colleagues and friends, to visit works that had since been constructed and for which he had been engaged in the preliminary surveying and planning, and to search for a lost love. It prompted me to recall some experiences that I had had during a career of more than half a century, as a civil engineer working both in the UK and overseas. As I made the transition into retirement, I contemplated the idea of possibly recording those experiences, before they faded from memory.

Having put it on the back burner for a while, two chance events coincided and re-awakened the idea. In 2017, during my tenure as Honorary Secretary of the Retired Members Section of the ICE's Yorkshire and Humber Region, I took part in a debate on the subject of rapidly advancing technologies and their impact on our profession, organised by the Institution's Graduates and Students Section. My contribution was to look back and explain how technologies had changed very considerably during my fifty plus years of professional practice, how engineers of my generation had embraced and utilised the new tools that became available to us over that period. I argued that, as we had done when the electronic calculator and the computer replaced the slide rule and tables of logarithms, so the current generation would adapt and thrive in a world of robotics and artificial intelligence, seeing them as tools to be used and not threats to the role of the engineer or employment opportunities.

At about the same time I learned that an acquaintance, Roger Barton, had written and published a book on his experiences of working in Africa[2]. Much of his time had been spent living in Malawi and journeying through Mozambique and Zimbabwe, countries that I had visited during the course of my employment. It occurred to me that if he could make a book out of his travels and experiences, so might I. On reading his book it became clear that, as well as making some ambitious journeys that I would not have attempted, he had a gift for observation, of understanding and explaining to the reader the life that he and the indigenous population lived. I doubt that I will reach his standard of erudition, but I hope that the reader will nevertheless find something of interest in my observations and anecdotes.

My sincere thanks therefore to Jack Moore and to Roger Barton for setting an example. My grateful thanks too to the many friends, colleagues and acquaintances whose paths crossed mine and enriched my professional life in one way or another, all of it starting from a fortuitous career opportunity that came my way in 1960.

In 2018, the Institution of Civil Engineers celebrated two hundred years since its formation in a London coffee shop. The Institution's first President was Thomas Telford, a name that must surely be known by many non engineers, not just those living in the town that was named after him. What Telford and others of similar stature achieved in their lifetimes have been recorded in biographies and other works of reference, but like the vast majority of civil engineers, I worked at a less exalted level. I didn't wish to fall into the trap of the Peter Principle[3] and was conscious of my own limitations. For potential recruits to the profession and young engineers starting out, notwithstanding considerable differences in the structure of today's industry and the tools and practices deployed, their experiences are more likely to be closer to mine than to the few who had the ability to rise to the very top of the profession.

The largest part of my working life was spent in the employment of one of the many medium-sized firms of consulting engineers. Based in the north of England, we tried hard to break into the big time, to be seen on a par and compete as equals with the national firms that had their headquarters in or around London and which had networks of local offices on the patches of provincial consultants like us. We had a few successes, but when eventually we were taken over by a larger company we had not quite succeeded in our ambition. We had however made some breakthroughs and could count a Queens Award for Export amongst our accomplishments. We were early adopters of the kinds of changes that the consulting engineering 'establishment' took longer to embrace, but in time they followed us down the same path.

In the 1960s and 70s, treatment facilities for water supply and sewage were generally described as "works". In the 80s and 90s they became "plants" and, in the case of the dirty water facilities, "sewage" became "wastewater". In references to such facilities I have generally used the format that applied to those installations at the time when I was involved with them.

There are many references to engineers and engineering. When capitalised as Engineer, the reference is to the formal position of a named person or firm given powers of supervision and administration within a legal contract, the parties to that contract being typically Employer and Contractor.

A considerable proportion of my professional output took the form of written documents of various kinds. I endeavoured to draft them in clear and correct English, since that is what clients and colleagues had a right to expect and were left behind in files and in project records when I departed for the next assignment. To achieve a standard that satisfied me, I was not averse to burning midnight oil that couldn't be logged on my time sheet.

Having been educated at a top Scottish state school, I naively believed that my command of the written word in English was pretty good, and certainly not inferior to an American of equivalent professional standing. I held that blinkered view until the 1990s when, on an assignment in Gaza, I came up against Bill Hoadley of that nationality, in his capacity as a senior manager in the United Nations Relief Works Agency (UNRWA) and our client representative for projects planned to improve the sanitation arrangements in the southern border town of Rafah. He scrutinised my reports with great thoroughness and, whilst he gave the attention that was needed to my technical appraisals and recommendations, he did not hold back from being 'picky' with my grammar and especially the incorrect use or absence of commas. Thanks Bill, you were right, I try my best to keep to your rules.

Every year on renewing my annual subscription to the Institution of Civil Engineers, I ticked a box that delivered a small contribution to the Institution's Benevolent Fund. I didn't give much thought to it and knew only that it helped out members who had fallen on hard times financially, especially those in later life. After a gap of many years I became re-acquainted with a former colleague who had worked for me in Leeds and in Iraq, I learned of the health problems that he had suffered and that he was being supported by the Fund.

The national press gave much coverage to the case of Tony Nicklinson, who was cruelly afflicted by 'locked-in' syndrome. Like me he was a civil engineer who had worked in the Middle East. I was pleased to learn that, as well as coming to the aid of my former colleague, the ICE's Benevolent Fund supported Tony and his family though those terribly difficult times. If a profit is derived from sales of this book it will go to that Fund.

Acknowledgements

Drafting a technical report or specification is one thing, compiling a book is quite another and I remain a novice in that business.

After I had roughed out a few chapters, I sent a copy to former colleague and latterly technical journalist, Bill McCann. He soon homed in on various stylistic fundamentals that needed attention. At that time it was by no means certain that my efforts would finally come to fruition as an actual published book, but as he didn't discourage me to the extent that he might well have done, perhaps not wanting to hurt my feelings, I put on my rose-tinted spectacles and pressed on. There are passages where I may well have reverted to the comfort zone of my natural style of writing; given a second opportunity, I expect Bill would have his blue pencil to hand.

I am especially grateful to my godson, James Falkingham, who, with considerable fortitude, waded through what was about the third version of this tome. Although it was substantially complete, it still exhibited too many shortcomings. He didn't hold back on identifying those that he found and while about it he made helpful suggestions on rewording. James I feel would have got on well with Bill from UNRWA.

John Haiste was a colleague for many years and we followed the same career pathway from engineering consultancy then to freelancer and expert witness; for much of the time we had the same employer. We both worked in Iraq and Romania and had similar encounters with the clients and authorities in those countries. John kindly cast his eye over the manuscript as it was nearing its final form. I am grateful to him for his comments and supplements to my anecdotes, reminding me of some details that I had forgotten, especially in the sections on Iraq, where he was resident for a time whereas I was just a visitor.

Tom Harkins is one of the current graduates in our profession, a cohort that impresses me with its enthusiasm and forward thinking approach. It is a view that I know is shared by my colleagues amongst the retirees. I thought it would be a good idea to let one of them loose on my draft, although it was with some trepidation that I waited for the feedback. I wasn't asking for a proof read, I needed to know if my narrative and the unfolding of events made sense to a reader whose world today is very different to the one in which I started out. Tom is employed in a different branch of the profession, so he could tell me if my ramblings on matters water and drainage had become submerged unintelligibly within my verbiage. He did what I asked of him and I thank him for both his general observations and specific remarks.

1 Beginnings

A Glasgow East Ender

If I am asked about my origins I say that I am a Glaswegian. I was born in a nursing home in that city, where my father and grandfather had also lived. Home however, was the large 1930s housing estate of Garrowhill, situated a mile or so beyond the Glasgow City boundary to the unfashionable east, on a parcel of land that was formerly in the ownership of J. M. Scott Maxwell of the Baillieston Estate. It is reported that Maxwell had been concerned about unrest in 1930s society, particularly the spread of Communism and Fascism, and it was his hope that through the sale of the land a community could be created where these movements would not hold much attraction for its residents[4].

Sandwiched between two main roads, to the north by the Glasgow to Edinburgh road, and to the south by the Glasgow to Airdrie road, Garrowhill was built by a single developer, Henry Boot & Co. of Sheffield. House bricks were made in Boot's own brickworks nearby. For us as children, the grounds which surrounded the kilns and stock yards provided what today would be regarded as unacceptably risky adventure play opportunities. The water that collected in the pits and quarries were sources of minnows to be captured in jam jars and frog spawn to be studied as they became tadpoles, very few of which survived into adult froghood.

The estate had two parades of shops, a church, presided over by the Reverend Kinnis, whose deep and booming voice at Sunday services was able to reach all corners of the auditorium without any need for amplification, and a primary school which I attended between the ages of five and eleven. The church and school were situated at the highest point of the estate, near to Maxwell's former mansion, Garrowhill House. The planners had wisely left a patch of sloping parkland in front of those premises, ideal for trying out our home-made pram wheeled 'bogies' and for sledging in the winter time after a fall of snow.

My father and grandfather were from the city's Dennistoun district, where they made their living as bakers. Helping out in the bake house and assisting Jimmy the van driver with his deliveries earned me some additional pocket money, and I did acquire a degree of proficiency in making donuts. Another job was floor cleaning. Although it was swept regularly of flour and loose spills, after a few days there was a build up of doughy deposits, well trodden in, like chewing gum on a footpath. I may have been the boss's son, but Mary, a long serving employee skilled in cake decoration, didn't hold back from delivering a few well chosen words in broad Glaswegian when my efforts with the scraper didn't come up to her standard.

To get from our home to Dennistoun, or to continue further into the city centre, one had to travel through the badlands of Shettleston, which in later years became known for all that was worst in Glasgow's run down east end. It is close by the huge 1950s council estates of Barlanark and Easterhouse which I recall being developed during my childhood, built to house families who had been displaced in slum clearance programmes elsewhere in the city. At the time Shettleston didn't seem to me to be an area to be avoided, we took the tram there on Saturday mornings, unaccompanied by parents, to enjoy cowboy films and cartoons at the Odeon cinema. As a teenager I would cycle with a friend to the Formica table topped and banquette seated State Café, next to the district's other cinema of that name. There we mixed it with the local 'Teddie Boys', kitted out in their drape jackets, tight jeans and thick crepe soled shoes (aka 'brothel creepers').

Hamilton Academy

Garrowhill is now within the jurisdiction of Glasgow City Council, but then it was in the County of Lanarkshire, so when I passed the qualifying examinations (equivalent to the '11 plus' in England), as a pupil at Garrowhill Primary School the state secondary school choices for me were within the county, even though there were Glasgow Corporation senior schools that were easier to get to – a main tram route into the city passed close to our house. I obtained a place at Hamilton Academy, which at that time had a reputation for academic excellence. I looked forward to it as several friends from my primary school were also going there.

I was kitted out with the school uniform at Forsyth's outfitters' shop in Hamilton's Cadzow Street. The jacket was a size or two on the large side, but it had to last for more than a year. At the age of eleven I had not yet reached the height of five feet, so the jacket had to be accompanied with grey shorts, the bottom of the long jacket leaving only a few inches of trouser leg visible, above the long socks and puny knees. Long trousers could be worn only when the height limit had been reached, which being a slow grower took me longer than most.

The breast pocket of the blue blazer was embroidered in green with the school badge, recording its founding in the year 1588 and the school motto: *Sola Nobilitat Virtus* (Virtue Alone Ennobles). In the senior school, pupils perceived to be of suitable character were picked out to serve as house prefects, they wore blazers which had gold braided edging. Those blessed with sporting talents and who represented the school in the first teams, mainly in rugby and hockey, had blazers with a ribbon edging. In the sixth form I was amongst a group who continued to wear the standard school blazer, unadorned by any decoration, visible evidence of our place in the pecking order.

It was my father I remember who took me to buy the uniform, I knew that my mother was unwell, but I was never told how bad it was, so it came as a severe shock when, during my first year at that school, she died of cancer. I had some health issues of my own that had been quietly present as a child and they became more prominent as an adolescent, resulting in numerous absences from classes. My demeanour changed from that of a confident and happy youngster with many friends, to someone who became more introverted, lacking in self-confidence and a bit of a loner.

In the upper school I found myself with a group of fellow pupils in what I can best describe as a side stream. We were perceived as able enough to be allowed to stay on after reaching the minimum school leaving age of 15 years, but not amongst the high flyers, who were pushed hard to maximise their potential and thus maintain the school's high standing when the examination results were announced. At the end of it all I did just manage to scrape through with the minimum that I would have needed to apply for a university place, but no one from the school thought to suggest it. In the 1950s only about 5% of school leavers went on to study full time at a university or equivalent higher educational institution.

Hamilton Town Council

My father had the idea of my becoming an accountant and had me lined up to be a trainee with the small firm that did the bakery's books. Not being terribly enthused by that career prospect, I recall trips to the library to try to find out about what other kinds of work I might prefer. An advertisement in the Hamilton Advertiser caught my eye – the Burgh Surveyor was looking to employ an apprentice civil engineer. Such a job had not come up in my searches up to that point, but a bit of digging soon revealed that it could encompass working with plans and maps. Since I was good at geography, liked maps and had contemplated becoming a surveyor of some kind, it seemed to me at the time that being a civil engineer might be the next best thing.

After a nervy interview I got the job offer: a salary of £260 per year with annual increments on the local authority scale, a 5½ day working week and 3 weeks annual paid holiday leave. It came with a formal indentured apprenticeship to James (Jimmy) White, the Burgh Surveyor, with day release and evening classes at technical college. It was paid employment for me, but senior engineers then could recall starting their apprenticeships without remuneration in their first year, having to continue relying on parental financial support until they were deemed to have reached a position of delivering net useful output for the employing organisation.

It was 1960 and the conscription of school leavers into military service under the National Service programme was ending, but the swinging and permissive '60s were still ahead of us and the culture and norms of the 1950s lingered on for a while.

The Surveyor's Department had the policy of starting a new junior every couple of years and on the first day I was introduced to my predecessor. He was delighted to see me, since he was then able to pass on all of the office junior tasks that had been his responsibility hitherto. Ronnie Simpson showed me the ropes and I quickly learned that he had another string to his bow, namely that of musicians' agent and event promoter.

The senior engineer in the drawing office, David Alexander, was notionally in charge, but he was not exactly a disciplinarian. Affectionately known to us as DA, in a nod to a popular men's hair style of the day, for the most part he turned a blind eye to Ronnie spending much time on the office telephone, organising his gigs. Highlights of the town's entertainment scene, Ronnie's events were held in the concert hall of the town's fine municipal building, on the floor above the lower ground floor office where we toiled away at our drawing boards (well toil is a bit of an exaggeration, this was 1960s local authority culture, but nevertheless we did do an honest day's work). Almost all of the younger employees in the building looked forward to going to Ronnie's concerts – he engaged top bands from England such as Chris Barber, Kenny Ball and Terry Lightfoot. Popular too were local favourites, the Clyde Valley Stompers. Their rendering of Prokofiev's *Peter and the Wolf* was a surprise pop hit[5]. It was the peak of the trad jazz craze, before it was ended abruptly by the Beatles and the Mersey Sound in 1963.

The world of work was an eye opener in meeting adult characters who fell well outside my zone of familiarity until then. David and Joe were intermediate level engineers, studying for their Higher National Certificates and the additional 'endorsement' subjects that they needed to pass in order to gain exemption from the Part 1 and Part 2 examinations of the Institution of Civil Engineers. If they cleared that hurdle, they could then proceed to the professional interview which was the final stage in achieving Chartered Engineer status. Both were from Glasgow and they commuted to and from Hamilton daily.

David and Joe were Protestant and Roman Catholic respectively. Then and sadly still now, fostered in part by the state education system, the religious divide was marked – it didn't take long after being introduced to someone to establish which foot he or she kicked with, the name could be a give-away, or just the way of pronouncing certain words and of course the school attended, if that came up in conversation. I had been personally affected by it as a child and I knew of the hate and coarse language that could be generated.

Whilst they retained their strong beliefs, it did not stop them enjoying each other's company in nights out at local bars and engaging in friendly banter with lots of point scoring. It helped perhaps that, whilst Joe was a keen Glasgow Celtic fan, David came from Partick and supported the Thistle, which was not the enemy to a follower of the Parkhead team in the same mould as those from Ibrox and Glasgow Rangers. They were fellow conspirators in introducing me to the ritual of bolting down a 'Wee Heavy' followed by a 'Glayva' so as to get properly tanked before the bar called time at 10.00 pm, in accordance with the local licensing laws that were then in force.

Our work stations were drawing boards with high chairs, with tables alongside to lay out plans etc. If one was lucky the drawing board was a purpose made free standing item, with a parallel motion straight edge that was operated by a system of pulleys, wires and weights. The more rudimentary variety simply comprised a piece of block board laid on a pair of substantial wedge shaped timber supports, mounted on a table top, with a manual T square. Lumps of solid lead wrapped with masking tape were used to keep a pile of drawings flat.

In the office we wore beige coloured linen coats, rather like short dressing gowns, to protect our clothes from ink stains. They would be personalised to a degree – David's had sergeants' stripes on the sleeve. Wearing a particularly well cut coat and a man of style was Tom Purdie, an older gentleman and not an engineer but a town planner by training. He was capable of producing examples of very fine quality draughtsmanship and it was to him that I was directed to learn from the master the techniques of drawing with pencil and with ink pens, the use of stencils, and the development of my own 'fist' of lettering by hand.

A skill that I appreciated learning from him, and enjoyed if I was tasked with it, was that of colouring drawings that were to be used for presentation purposes, to take to Council meetings or for public display. Mixing the solid colour sticks with water in small ceramic dishes, careful application and a steady hand was needed to keep exactly to the edge lines.

Tom's hobby was breeding budgerigars and he brought them into work, not in cages but in his illustrations. He could happily while away a tea or lunch break sketching examples of his beloved birds, in correct colouring and in various poses. He had a similar ability with the female form and if he got a bit bored with sketching yet another winged bird he would create a seductive image in skimpy lingerie or swimwear. Esquire might have been his magazine of choice.

He had a sporting Sunbeam Rapier saloon, in two tone cream and red, always kept spotlessly clean both outside and in. Heaven for Tom would have been attending a get together of fellow budgerigar fanciers in his car, accompanied by one of his imagined coterie. She might oblige by draping herself over its bonnet in the style that typically featured in motor trade calendars of that era, generally to be found pinned on the walls of garage workshops.

A new broom

In the second year of my employment at the Council, Jimmy White was faced with the task of recruiting a replacement for his deputy, a gentleman of the old school who was approaching retirement. Mr Rennie had his own office and we didn't see a lot of him. A new regime began when, over the head of David Alexander, David Blair took up residence in the drawing office, pending a move into the deputy's office when it was vacated by Mr Rennie.

The prior comfortable environment was disrupted as the new man exerted his authority. He had a tendency to make remarks about staff which he regarded as mildly humorous, but they were just as likely to hit a nerve as they would the funny bone.

His love for his Volkswagen car and the scorn which he poured on the family saloons coming out of British factories was frequently expressed to anyone who cared to listen. In 1961, the only model of VW, the legendary beetle, was joined by a larger saloon that was based on similar rear-engined principles, the mundanely named and much less successful 1500. With some glee he announced to us all that this would be the final nail in the coffin of the British motor industry. By this and other means he fostered a 'them and us' environment in the office. As he was also small in stature he was soon nicknamed "Little Hitler".

He could not have been expected to foresee that, a few years later, VW was to abandon air cooled engines that were hung out over the driven rear axle, in favour of the polar opposite approach that was pioneered by Alec Issigonis and the British Motor Corporation and then widely adopted by car manufacturers worldwide.

In the 1960s and through to the 80s, the female gender in engineering offices was represented almost solely by secretarial and admin or accounts staff. An exception was the job of tracer, which was wholly female, although tracers were not employed at Hamilton. The main focus of our fantasies and ribaldry on an everyday level was on the two departmental secretaries, Ethel and Sheena. Ethel was the older of the two and would take a certain amount of innuendo with good humour, but had a line that should not be crossed. Sheena was my age and had had a strict Roman Catholic upbringing. She was an attractive girl with a happy disposition, but made it clear that she wouldn't stand for any attempt to flirt, by dismissive laughter and throw-away lines as she smartly turned on her heel and left the male macho environment that was our office.

Taking over from Ronnie as office 'gofer', I don't recall it being unduly onerous or tedious; my abiding memory of working in that office for two years is of gaining a sound grounding in civil engineering. The schemes that were devised in the office were generally small, but since in that era municipalities like Hamilton had responsibility for roads, water, drainage, refuse and street lighting, the opportunity to learn a few basics in all of these fields was extremely valuable and I look back on the experience most favourably.

The mausoleum and the motorway

An unusual task that I was asked to perform was to check the settlement of the 10th Duke of Hamilton's mausoleum, since it was being affected by mining subsidence. Sometimes known as "Il Magnifico", it is a unique building – the chapel has a dome some 36 metres in height and has 'whispering alcoves'. The doors are of massive cast bronze, surface modelled in bas relief with such quality and craftsmanship that one can place a finger behind the head of a figure and feel features on the other side, modelled just as if it had been visible from the front.

Settlement in the vertical plane was not a problem, but if it was uneven, causing the building to tilt, that was a cause for concern. Plumb bobs on wires were hung from pins on the frieze below the dome, and the extent of out of verticality was measured and monitored over time. For obvious reasons it needed to be done on a windless day.

If you have driven past Hamilton along the M74 motorway it is doubtful that you will have given much thought to its route planning. In 1961 the engineers at the Department of Transport had spent much time and effort in this endeavour and they devised three possible alignments for the proposed motorway, denoted as the red, blue and green route options. The Town Council was duly invited to choose one of them. However none found favour with the councillors, a key objection being that all three resulted in the mausoleum being cut off from the rest of the town, albeit remaining within the municipal boundary, which was the River Clyde to the east. Although it was a Labour controlled council, the councillors saw themselves as caretakers of the town's history and that included the mausoleum, which had been built at great expense for a wealthy and privileged aristocrat.

Jimmy White took a look at the plans and it didn't take him long to come up with a fourth option, one which he explained to councillors would be more expensive due the poorer ground conditions that could be expected, being closer to the river and in its flood plain. To assist the councillors in their deliberations it was decided to set out the routes marked by coloured poles along each of the alignments. On the day of inspection we were out early with a team of labourers from the Burgh Yard, the councillors were then driven around in cars to observe the routes from various vantage points. It was no surprise to us that the councillors were unanimous in rejecting the red blue and green and chose Jimmy's yellow route.

How the Provost and Town Clerk won the day with the Scottish Office I have no idea, but win it they did. As it passes Hamilton, the mausoleum being just visible through the trees, the M74 follows roughly the yellow route, hastily put together in our office in a fraction of the time spent by the 'men from the ministry' in devising their unsuccessful options.

In later years, having moved to Leeds to find employment there, I was a regular traveller along the M74 motorway which now by-passes Hamilton and into which there was no particular reason for me to go, as either I was close to my destination heading north, or had just left it heading south. A friend and fellow Italian car enthusiast, who lived in the neighbouring small town of Uddingston[6], invited me to accompany him at a classic car display in the town centre's pedestrianised shopping streets. So in 2016 I joined him there with my 1973 Alfa Romeo. More than 50 years had passed and I wanted to visit a few old haunts, including the mausoleum.

The building had been fenced off to protect it from vandals, but the pins for the plumb bobs were still visible. The original bronze doors had been removed and placed inside the main chamber, where they can still be seen by visitors on open days. Their replacements on the outside are made from oak. I went to the nearby museum where they were also custodians of the mausoleum and I learned that they did still monitor the settlement, although mining activity has long since ceased. The mausoleum had settled an estimated 6 metres in total, but the tilt was barely discernible.

Perks and politics

A perk of the job as the junior engineer in the office was to draw up plans for what were termed Minor Warrants. The most common scenario was of a resident of the town coming into the planning office to seek permission to erect a garage. To accompany the application, a plan of the site was required, together with a simple plan, elevation and cross section of the building. If you don't have anyone to draw it up, we might have someone in the office willing to do it for you, on a private basis and for a modest fee, they were informed. A number of applicants took up that offer and it generated some additional pocket money. Professional indemnity insurance was an unknown concept to me at that time!

I had been in Hamilton, both at school and then at work, and I was not disinterested in the local politics. I was aware that Scottish nationalism was experiencing a renaissance in the town – a few years later Winifred Ewing startled the pundits by winning the 1967 Hamilton parliamentary election for the Scottish National Party (SNP). She was only the second SNP Member of Parliament in its history, the first having been Robert McIntyre, who in 1945 was elected for the adjacent Motherwell constituency.

In 1959 there was a general election which was won nationally by the Conservatives, with Harold Macmillan as Prime Minister. The school's debating society held a mock election where a future Member of the Scottish Parliament and a bit of a rebel within her party, Margo Macdonald, was the SNP 'candidate'. A striking figure with long blond hair, she had a forceful personality and persuaded me that I should cast my vote for her. A non conformist at school too, Margo was one of a group of girls who, after the rector (headmaster) admonished pupils who didn't adhere strictly to the school's blue & green uniform rules, reacted against his diktat by turning up in bright red stockings. Another future politico was Isobel Lindsay, who stood for the Communist Party in the mock election. I am unable to recall who stood for the Conservatives and for Labour, clearly they did not make as much an impression on me as those two girls did at the time.

Nationalism did hold some attraction for me then, for no particular reason other than it wasn't mainstream, but in later life, when travelling around other countries, I was content to be acknowledged as a Brit just as much as I was a Scot. I am more inclined now to take a negative view of the kind of politics that emphasises differences and fosters divisions that would otherwise take less damaging forms.

In the summer of 2014, a few weeks before the referendum on Scottish independence, I was in Prague for a few days. Close to the hotel was a bar where I went one evening for a nightcap, it had an impressive selection of whiskies on display and I chose my tipple. The young barman was energetic, in the manner of Tom Cruise in the 1988 film 'Cocktail', and in between his manoeuvres and dealing with other customers we chatted. It transpired that he was a Slovak from Banská Bystrica, a pleasant town in the centre of the country that I had visited once.

I mentioned about the upcoming Scottish referendum and I probably had a whinge that I was barred from voting since I was living in England, whereas an expatriate Scot living in Prague was able to do so, by retaining a vote in the Scottish constituency where he or she had previously lived. An electoral role that was used in parliamentary elections was adopted for the referendum on nationhood, in my view inappropriately, simply as it was the easiest thing to do.

He would have been a babe in arms when, after the fall of communism, Czechoslovakia divided to become the Czech and Slovak Republics. I asked him what he thought about the collective decision of his forebears, expecting him to hold forth on how he was a proud Slovak etc. "Pah" was the essence of his response, "stupid thing promoted by politicians who had their own agenda, wanted to be bigger fish in a smaller pool, etc." I rather wish that Margo could have been there while I sat back and listened to their debate.

2 A University Education

The Royal College

After two years with the Burgh Surveyor I was settled into a civil engineering career, my goal then being to achieve chartered status through part time academic study concurrently with employment, a well trodden route. But change was coming. The Institution of Civil Engineers decided that, in future, the university degree entry route was to be favoured. The writing was on the wall and so I made the decision to move onto that pathway and apply for a university place as a full time student.

Although by then I had acquired an Ordinary National Certificate (ONC) in engineering, 'with distinction', it was my school examinations at the higher leaving certificate that got me in. I had hoped that my ONC would give me exemption from the first year of the four year degree course, but it wasn't counted. I had to start in the first year, where I found that much of the syllabus was familiar ground and I sailed through it.

Whereas nowadays it is the norm for an undergraduate to depart the childhood nest and study in another city as part of the process of maturing into an adult, in Scotland then it was more common to live at home and attend the local university, if one lived within commuting distance. The relationship that I had with my father was not close and I was reluctant to ask him to fund my living away from home. Since I was no longer earning a salary, he would have to grant me a small living allowance. That was doable for him if I remained at home, where I had my board and lodging provided. Thus my Glasgow choice was between the eponymous university and the Royal College of Science and Technology.

The latter institution was regarded as being equivalent to a university and the qualification awarded at the end of the four year undergraduate course was Associate of the Royal College (ARCST). An ARCST opened just as many doors into employment as a BSc from Glasgow University and was recognised by the ICE. As it was easier to get to from my home and I preferred the look of syllabus, I chose it. In my final year at RCST there were radical changes in tertiary education, when a number of polytechnics were elevated to university status. The Royal College felt that it could not continue with its historical name and so it re-badged itself as the University of Strathclyde.

Reference to badges reminds me of the dress code. Engineering students, virtually all of whom were male, generally attended lectures in sports jacket and collared shirt with tie, but a significant minority turned out in a blazer with the college badge on the breast pocket and with matching tie, just as they had worn at secondary school.

At the College I encountered foreigners for the first time, students from other parts of Europe, Africa and Asia. At the age of 20 I had never been on a foreign holiday. Those who had come from the Indian sub-continent generally already had a degree from a local university. But that was not regarded with the same esteem as one from a British university, to advance their careers it was a good move to come to the UK and obtain a degree here.

In the 1950s and early 60s one rarely encountered a black person in Scotland. Immigration from our former colonies had been rather limited in a part of the UK that didn't offer much attraction by way of job prospects. Sunday Adigun was the first African that I came to know, studying civil engineering as l was. He was a Nigerian from a well off family, his father being a tribal chief or elder. Sunday was a tall man of striking appearance with three scars on each facial cheek denoting his tribal origin. Always with a broad smile on greeting, he was good company.

People of oriental origin were not unknown in Scotland, but my personal exposure hitherto had been limited to being waited on in a Chinese restaurant. Chan was from Hong Kong and in our informal social group. He owned a Renault Dauphine, a rear-engined motor with a certain chic appeal, perceived to be more of a lady's car. I was into cars by then and liked tinkering with the mechanical bits. I did have a motor cycle when at Hamilton, but having come off it three times and having walked away unscathed on each occasion, I thought it was unwise to push my luck any further and so in a shared ownership scheme with a friend I bought an 'old banger' with four wheels, one that required regular attention to keep it going. Chan's Dauphine was not the most reliable of vehicles either and as he wasn't as mechanically minded as I was and didn't have anywhere to work on it, he brought it to our house where we had a garage, work bench and tools. I did manage to effect some improvement, at least for a while, and he kept it for the duration of his stay.

Working at Hamilton Town Council for two years had to some extent brought me out of the shell of my introversion and I gained in confidence at Royal College, aided by my being older than fellow students who had arrived straight from school, having that understanding of the subject matter that two years of work experience had given me. Gap years were unheard of then. Some students dropped out when they struggled with the study, or concluded that they had made the wrong choice. One of the latter who I befriended for the first year was Stuart (Stu) from Hessle, near Hull. He was desperate to get into the Royal Air Force and in the meantime was studying engineering. His self confidence and raffish persona seemed an ideal fit for a career in that service, and as if that wasn't enough of a head start in life, his looks were straight from the pages of a fashion magazine, Stu was truly a girl magnet.

Much of the social life at the college revolved around the Students' Union. During the lunch break we re-energised ourselves with the mainly greasy spoon fare that was served up in the refectory. Burgers were made in advance of the lunch break and were kept warm and soggy within their buns in old biscuit tins. Sausage rolls, Forfar bridies, mutton pies, chips and beans completed the menu on offer.

To pass the time during the lunch break I was in a card school with a small group of fellow would be civil engineers, two Davids and an Ian, whose twin sister I was rather attracted to but didn't have the confidence to ask out. A hugely popular diversion was the daily film show that regularly featured Tom and Jerry cartoons. The original and classic T&Js that were produced by Fred Quimby, head of MGM's animation studio, were greeted with rousing acclaim when his name appeared in the credits before the action. But after his retirement Hanna and Barbera of Flintstones fame took over the role and with it came a change in animation style and story lines that was less frantic and anarchic. These were not to our liking and were booed.

The annual highlight was the college ball, at which men wore dinner suits and girls attended in glamorous evening dresses. It was a long and alcohol fuelled evening that went on into the early hours. By this time I had a first girl friend, Fiona, later to become my wife. Her mother was a dressmaker and seamstress, a sheath tight red sequined number is etched in my memory. Fiona was fashion conscious and could carry it off at such an event.

Red Road Flats

Engineering students were encouraged to find summer employment of some kind in a relevant engineering environment. During the first vacation I got a job with Redpath Brown, a firm of structural steel fabricators and erectors. I was informed at interview that the primary requirement for the job was experience and competence in the use of surveying instruments, which I had. Convenient for travel, being east of the city centre and only a few miles from my home, the Red Road flats were the highest structural steel framed dwellings in Europe at that time and they were mid way through their construction. There were eight blocks in total and the work had been split between two companies, four blocks each.

I arrived on site on the first day and was astonished to see that a number of guy ropes had been attached to the side of one of the tower blocks, in a sight reminiscent of Gulliver. I reported to Redpath's site foreman who informed me that this was the imperfect erection of rival firm Flemings. The means of correcting its diversion from the desired vertical plane was to slacken off bolts connecting the columns and beams and then to pull it back into alignment using the steel ropes and winches.

Redpath's foreman had no doubt about his blocks, but my first task was to check it with the theodolite – there had been an engineer on site at the start of the job to set out the bases, but not since then, all of the erection having been executed subsequently using plumb bobs and spirit levels. It didn't take me long to perform the check and to find that he was right, and I reported thus back to head office. Suitably impressed and with that job done in the first day, I enquired what more might be required of me.

I found out then why he had asked for an engineer with instrument competence. He didn't need me to tell him that the frames were going up in correct fashion, although his superiors in the office wanted to be sure of it, but he was finding that the task of levelling up the angle brackets used to support the external cladding panels was rather time consuming. He was using a combination of tape measure and water filled U tubes. It would be so much simpler and quicker, he suggested, if I set up my level in the middle of the floors, once they had been concreted, and worked with the erectors to fix and tighten the bolts.

I was fortunate that my instrument stations were in the middle of the floors as I didn't have a head for heights (I question now why I even took the job!). So apart from helping out with some paperwork in the site cabin, that was my role for two months, day in day out, not a lot of variation. I came to respect greatly the foreman and his erector team, who worked together harmoniously under his competent direction. They relied upon and had to trust one another with their lives.

There was nothing wrong with the engineering that went into the Red Road flats, but the same cannot be said of their management. Years of neglect took their toll and fifty years after their erection it was decided that they were beyond salvation, so they were scheduled for demolition. I suppose that the original scheme promoters at the time would not have been dismissive of the suggestion that they may have a 50 year life, it was conventional practice in those days to make comparisons of scheme options on the basis of loan repayments of 30 or 40 years for buildings. In the end there was a mad idea to make a feature of the demolition as part of the spectacle of the opening ceremony of the 2014 Commonwealth Games. I am glad that that plan was scotched, as it would have done a disservice to the engineers and others who contributed to their creation and who were not to blame for their decline.[7]

Dunbartonshire County Council

In a second year of summer employment I had a job with Dunbartonshire County Council, quite a long way from home, but as weekends were often being spent at a family caravan at Rosneath, on Gareloch, it was convenient enough for Fridays and Mondays. Again at interview I was asked about my experience with instruments, not of the surveying type this time but drawing office instruments. Once more it was my basic training in Hamilton Town Council that secured it for me. I was warmly welcomed by my new colleagues, I was needed to catch up with a backlog that had developed in the production of bills of quantities for a new highway scheme.

On my desk was a deep pile of drawings of longitudinal and cross sections of the proposed road. The quantities of excavation cut and embankment fill had to be calculated and that entailed hour upon hour upon hour with the planimeter[8] and slide rule. The senior engineers did recognise the monotony of the job and so from time to time I was invited to go with them on a site visit to inspect some works under construction or to carry out a condition survey, but I don't recall coming away from the two month assignment having learned anything new.

The general atmosphere in the office was very much nine to five and with not a great deal of enthusiasm displayed. I marked it down as a place I would not think to apply for post graduate employment. The only recollection I have now of my colleagues there is of Debabrata, a Hindu; we would sometimes go out for lunch together and he confided in me that he was rather partial to corned beef.

Buchanan's Whisky Bottling Plant

In the third summer I took a break from civil engineering. Dick, or Richard Lionel Liversedge, to give him his full name, was the boyfriend of my girlfriend's widowed aunt. He was a Liverpudlian working in Glasgow as export sales manager for James Buchanan & Co., the Scotch whisky distillers. He was well suited to that role, having both a love of the company's fine product and a salesman's gift with words, great company to be with on any social occasion. Dick offered to get me a job in their bottling plant and bonded warehouse in Glasgow, near the docks. It was labouring pure and simple, the money was good and I had more than sufficient civil engineering work experience to put in front of a prospective employer after graduation.

Like my two previous summer jobs, there was a substantial element of routine about it and risk of boredom, but I learned a trick or two that would never have come my way in a civil engineering workplace. On the first day I was taken into the loading bay area where flat bed trucks reversed in from the street outside and were loaded up with cases of whisky, by hand, no fork lift trucks or pallets were used. The foreman introduced me to Hector, a large and muscular man. Hector will train you he said. I watched for a bit how the cases were stacked onto the lorry and wondered what the training entailed.

"Pick up that case" said Hector. I did so, and was conscious of its weight. "Did no one ever teach you how to lift a box son?" If they had I must have forgotten. He stooped, grasped a case with his two hands on opposing corners, diagonally, and lifted it. "This is how, now you try it." I did so and agreed that it was easier that way. "OK, that's you trained, just follow me and the others in how we place the boxes on the back of the truck." And so I did and continued in that loading bay for two months, being thankful that I had the prospect of more stimulating employment in the years to come.

It is not difficult to appreciate the temptation that is represented by the vast quantities of distilled liquor that are held within such a facility. In an effort to keep illicit activities to a minimum, a ration of whisky was dispensed twice a day, morning and afternoon, for those who wished to partake of it. One would line up and, in a 'down the hatch' manner, quickly consume whatever was on offer and then go straight back to work. The origins of that spirit generally did not come from filled bottles or from bulk casks, but from plant maintenance operations. If there was a problem on a bottling line it may prove necessary to drain some liquor from the system. If there was no contamination, that spirit was not simply bled off to waste but was collected and used for the daily ration. Whiskies of all ages and strengths passed through the plant, from deluxe 12 year olds to low strength 3 year spirit that was destined for certain markets. One never knew in the ration line-up what would be dispensed on a given occasion.

Notwithstanding the twice daily official ration, employees at the plant deployed various methods to release a few more drams illegitimately. Motivation was just as much in the plotting and execution and getting one over on the management as it was in the consumption. One method that was used sparingly, since over-use would be *prima face* evidence of deliberate intent, was the dropped case. The cases containing twelve bottles of whisky were of stout corrugated cardboard, which gave reasonable protection to the bottles in transit, but not if a case was dropped onto a concrete floor from wagon load bed height.

The contents of a broken bottle would seep through the cardboard, which acted as a filter to block any shards of broken glass. If by some good fortune there was a small container to hand, the escaping liquor may as well be captured rather than it running away to waste. So as not to overdo things, and to increase the chance of success, a case would be dropped such that a corner bottle took the full force of the impact and was more likely to break, whilst leaving the others intact. It's something that comes to mind occasionally if I'm in a wine merchant's emporium, but knowledge that I keep to myself.

Carswells

Many students sought temporary employment during the Christmas and New Year break, . The Post Office was a favourite, but its need for additional hands came to an end after Christmas Day. With another student I worked in the knitwear department of what was known then as gentlemen's outfitters. Think Grace Brothers in "Are You Being Served?" and you would be on the right general lines. We did have an equivalent of Captain Peacock, although not a Miss Brahms or a Mrs Slocombe. Carswells was situated within Glasgow's prime retail shopping area, on the corner of Renfield Street and St Vincent Street.

As young men we would be directed especially to serve girls of our age group looking to purchase good quality branded sweaters and cardigans for a boyfriend or brother, it being expected that they would relate to us more readily than to the store's permanent employees who were generally a bit older.

The store took pride in delivering a good quality shopping experience to its middle class clientele. Part of that was the careful wrapping of the purchased goods from a large roll of heavyweight brown paper, tied up with tape which was embroidered with the shop's name. Learning to fold a sweater or cardigan carefully so that it slid nicely back into the makers sleeve and then present it into a neat parcel was a skill that required some practice to acquire. It has served me well every Christmas and birthday since.

Hydraulic leanings

The first two years at RCST were spent studying general engineering and not much of that was civil. Only in the third year did we part company from our mechanical and electrical colleagues and become fully embraced by the Department of Civil Engineering. I soon discovered that my interest lay in the field of hydraulics and I was fortunate that senior lecturer, Alan Smith, presided over an excellent course which provided a sound grounding in the subject.

In my final year I had to choose an item of research and prepare a thesis, I was overseen in this respect by Professor Ian Barr, a true boffin and a gentle man. At the time he was interested in some work being done by American academic, Dr Garbis Keulegan, and had embarked on a programme of tests of his own to verify and extend the results of the behaviour of fluids of different density when one was introduced into the other. An example could be the discharge of warm (less dense) water from a power station into a river or lake of cold (more dense) water. Salinity intrusion was another.

I conducted many trials in the hydraulics lab and for my thesis I reported and analysed the results and their implications on the theories and formulae that had been postulated to date. Whether my efforts were of significant value I never found out, but Barr was happy enough with them to count towards my degree.

3 Crouch and Hogg

The design office

During my final year I was introduced to the idea of obtaining a research assistant's post and studying for a PhD, but undecided I did the rounds of potential employers who were looking to recruit fresh graduates. Babtie Shaw and Morton was by far the largest firm of consulting engineers in Scotland at the time and I did get a job offer from them, but I decided to join one of their rivals, Crouch and Hogg, since it provided the opportunity of working on the design of Scotland's largest ever water project, the Loch Lomond Water Supply Scheme, for the Central Scotland Water Development Board.

I started sitting my finals in June of 1966, but after the first two or three papers I experienced severe abdominal pains on the Friday of the first week. Admitted to Glasgow's Royal Infirmary, the cause of my discomfort was soon diagnosed and in short order I was wheeled into the operating theatre where I had my appendix removed. By the Monday I felt that I was recovering well and was wondering if an arrangement could be made for me to sit the next examinations in the hospital, under supervision.

My lecturer in soil mechanics, Alan McGowan, came into visit. Even if the university administration could facilitate it, I could not possibly be in as fit and prepared a condition as I was before the incident, he warned, and I would risk a degree classification that would be poorer as a result. Take the examinations next year, he said, you will be free to come into the university whenever you wish, no additional fees to be paid (by my local authority in those days), the academic staff would assist me as much as they could.

I took his good advice. Crouch and Hogg kindly agreed to employ me in their Glasgow office on the offered terms and put me onto their ICE training scheme, on the understanding that I would sit and be expected to pass the university's examinations in a year's time.

On my first day I was given the small task of designing an anchoring arrangement for the raw water inlet to a new water treatment plant for the town of Galashiels in the Scottish borders. The source of water was a loch at much higher elevation and a special Larner-Johnson energy dissipation valve was to be fitted at the end of the pipeline where it entered the plant. High forces were generated, hence the need for the anchor to resist them.

There was already a design prepared, but it didn't find favour with the office's senior engineer who was in charge of the project, he wanted me to devise something better. It had been done by my immediate predecessor, a fellow student of mine at the RCST who, having been awarded his first class honours degree, decided to change tack and take the research assistant's post that was on offer there. George Fleming went on to have a distinguished career, leaving behind the design of pipe anchorages and becoming an expert in the computer simulation of floods and sediment transport. An Emeritus Professor at the University of Strathclyde, he reached the top of the profession when in 1999 he was elected President of the Institution of Civil Engineers.

I took some holiday leave before the 1967 examinations for preparation and revision, and regarded myself as fortunate to have been awarded an honours degree, first class. The episode had put paid to any thought of returning to academia and pursuing research and PhD. A year on and I was enjoying the work of the design office and on a path that should lead to chartered status.

My father had a number of pastimes, in sporting and practical fields, and in all of those spheres he was more accomplished than I. He had been a keen amateur photographer at one time and had gained awards at his local camera society, being especially noted for his fine portrait studies. At my graduation he brought his camera for the obligatory shot, in my gown and clutching my degree certificate, made out in Latin on heavyweight cartridge paper and encased in its red tube. Untypically for him he did not frame the shot with the care that could have been expected. I like to think that he was overcome with pride at my achievement, which accounts for the unfortunate positioning in front of a drainage manhole cover, a portent of things to come.

Having graduated and with my job secure, it was time to leave home and start anew with my own place, or more correctly our place, as Fiona and I were married in the November of that year. Although in 1967 the 60s were swinging in London, in Presbyterian and middle class society in Scotland, living together was just not an option. I can recall my father's horror when the son of a good friend of his 'had to get married' after his girlfriend became pregnant.

Like virtually every other firm of consulting engineers at the time, Crouch and Hogg was a traditional partnership, i.e. the whole of the equity was owned in varying proportions by the partners. There were senior and junior partners. The senior partners were those who had been there for some time and held the majority of the equity. The junior partners were younger and were in the process of buying into the firm, a senior partner would retire by selling out his share. Below the partners in hierarchy were a number of associates, senior engineers who were in line for a partnership when the next opportunity arose.

This model was workable when income was based on the standard scales of fees published by the Association of Consulting Engineers (ACE); they were pitched at a level that could earn a partner a very comfortable living. ACE members were not permitted to compete openly with one other on the basis of fee, but solely on the basis of technical competence and experience. It was argued that this model maintained high professional standards, as there was no financial incentive to give work to a less qualified firm. It was a closed shop, but the predominantly public sector clients did not query the arrangement. ACE members would be at pains to point out that they complied with a strict code of ethics under which clients could be assured of their independence from any commercial influences. An ACE member getting into bed with a contractor on a design and construct project was a rarity at that time.

Design of the huge Loch Lomond scheme was divided up into several sections, mine came under junior partner, George Milne, and associate, Hugh Speed, but that project was just one of several that were under way in the section. The firm had a long standing presence in the Scottish borders area and had a local office there. The projects were mostly concerned with water supply, but others came our way which I had an opportunity to work on. One of those was a new factory built at Jedburgh for the American L S Starrett Company, which made saw blades and other tools. Checking fifty years later, I was pleased to find that Starretts are still very much in business and that Jedburgh remains the centre of their UK and European operations. A better result than the Red Road flats.

There were a good many trips to the borders, many being with George Milne, who drove us there in his Volvo 'Amazon' estate car. It had some wear in the transmission and a definite clunk could be felt at gear changes as slack in the several linkages was taken up from neutral into drive mode. George enjoyed smoking a pipe, which required refilling at least once on the journey. That would be executed on a convenient straight section of the road, without stopping the car, the steering wheel being held gently with his knees. Both hands were required to open the tobacco tin, remove a ring of the compressed product, rub it into a nice friable consistency in the palm of the hand, then, while holding the bowl of the pipe, placing and compacting the tobacco into it to the required density. The subsequent lighting operation could be performed single handed with the pipe clamped between the teeth, the other hand being on the steering wheel. In fairness to George, who sadly passed away in 2015, there was much less traffic in the 1960s than there is today.

With a considerable client base throughout Scotland, one could be despatched on assignments some distance from the office, necessitating overnight stops. The small fishing town of Buckie on the north-east coast was one of those and I was charged with the job of undertaking a survey in connection with some proposed drainage works. I enquired of a secretary where we would normally stay in the town and she thought that the Marine Hotel had been used, so on my request she booked me in there. On return to the office, feeling satisfied that I had concluded the task satisfactorily, I was called into George's office for what I assumed would be a de-briefing. Instead it was to be admonished for staying at the Marine Hotel, which was where the senior partner, Mr Carnie, stayed on his visits. Staff, he advised me, should stay at the Commercial Hotel. As I had not been to blame it would be overlooked this time, but I should check carefully before booking overnight stays in the future.

George Milne was a man for attention to detail and I found that I had a similar mindset. So I didn't object when one day he brought me some drawings of a treatment plant building that had been prepared by an architect and he drew my attention to the door and window details. "I don't think they have got this right" he said, as he explained how water penetration might occur, "see if you can design a damp proof course (DPC) detail that will work." I spent a happy day with DPCs, producing isometric views to show how they would be formed, at a cost to the firm well in excess of the pieces of waterproof membrane that would be deployed.

George had a healthy scepticism about architects, with whom he was polite and pleasant in meetings. His stance did rub off on me I think and in later years, when in charge of designs for treatment plant buildings that did not require any special aesthetic treatment, I decided on a style and with component catalogues to hand and assisted by technicians who were familiar with building works details, I produced what was necessary without involving an architect.

As the Loch Lomond scheme began to take shape I was given the job of designing a huge pumping station at the proposed Balmore Water Treatment Works, which is situated to the north of Glasgow. We were designing in imperial units so I will give its capacity in them – 100 million gallons per day, although not all of the pumps were to be installed in the first phase.

The hydraulic calculations that were needed through the treatment plant and its ancillary streams were reasonably challenging, but it was perceived wisdom at that time that a structure in reinforced concrete or steel was more likely to be considered favourably as being of sufficient substance to pass muster at the Institution's professional interview. I was therefore happy to have the job of designing the massive pumping station sub-structure in reinforced concrete. With it I could also produce a bill of quantities, another element of the professional interview package. Thus, after two years plus in the design office, I was some way along on the path towards chartered status.

The other essential component was a minimum of a year's experience on a construction site. The timing of the execution stage of the Balmore Water Treatment Works coincided nicely with my schedule, when Crouch and Hogg was staffing up to provide teams of engineers to supervise the construction contractors.

Balmore Water Treatment Works

On a hillside above the village of Balmore, one of the largest water treatment works in Scotland was constructed. Raw water is abstracted from Loch Lomond at Ross Priory and then pumped to Balmore. After treatment at Balmore, the water is then pumped eastwards and into various service reservoirs.

In a departure from the more conventional two stage process of clarification (settlement) followed by sand filters, Loch Lomond water was treated in a single stage using rotating microstrainers, which filtered out unwanted particles using a fabric woven from fine stainless steel wire. Everything was large scale, the works having its own 11 kV electricity sub-station. There were huge reinforced concrete tanks for the storage of raw and treated water.

The civil engineering and building works were undertaken by an English contractor, Mitchell Construction Ltd. Major players in the water industry, Glenfield and Kennedy and Wallace and Tiernan, provided the main items of process equipment. Harland Engineering of Alloa, later taken over by the Weir Group, supplied the main pumps.

The supervision team comprised the Resident Engineer (RE), myself as Assistant RE, a senior engineer who was responsible for the measurement of work in progress that formed the basis of monthly payments to the contractor, and two civil engineering inspectors, or clerks of works.

Our Resident Engineer was George T Stevenson, a gentleman from Jedburgh who was addressed as Mr Stevenson by his employers, the Crouch and Hogg partners, as well as those of us working under him. In conversation we referred to him simply as GT. He was at or past retirement age, but had been obliged to find employment of the kind that Crouch & Hogg were able to offer when his own small contracting company failed and with it his financial security. It was a reminder of the financial fragility of the construction side of the industry and for him a personal tragedy, which he bore without any outward display of bitterness.

As I came to learn many years later, in some other countries he would have been an obvious target for a contractor seeking an easier ride on the job in return for whatever inducements would be needed to achieve it. Whereas his opposite number, Mitchell Construction's site agent,

George Grattan, arrived and departed site in a new and sizeable motor car that was provided by the company, GT commuted every week the long distance from Jedburgh, close to the English border, in his small second hand Austin A40.

GT spent more of his time in his office than out on the site, we were his eyes and ears for the most part, but he did make routine tours of inspection and would quickly be on the case in person if needed to deal with a particular problem. He had a collection of stock phrases that applied in various situations, one of which was "like a dog p***ing in snow", deployed when, having examined the alignment of a long wall or footing, he concluded that it wasn't in a perfect straight line.

Having spent all of his life as a contractor, our boss was quick to identify any shortcomings in Mitchell's planning and working procedures. Excuses that were given for problems which arose that had a negative cost impact on Mitchells, and which were thought by them to provide grounds for a claim for additional costs, were given short shrift.

At the time Mitchell Construction had a contract at the massive Kariba Dam on the River Zambezi, which forms the border between Zambia and Zimbabwe (not the dam itself which was constructed by an Italian company). It was the company's halo project. Senior to the site agent at Balmore was the contracts manager, Vic Farthing, who had been Mitchell's agent at Kariba and as a consequence his standing in the company was high. His reputation preceded him and Mitchell's site staff were suitably deferential, however GT took a more sceptical line, credentials that derived from other projects carried little weight with him. This didn't go down terribly well, and whether it was that, or a job going satisfactorily that required only a light touch on the senior management tiller, the contracts manager was not a frequent visitor to Balmore.

GT was keen to maintain the psychological upper hand over the contractor at all times. The RE was also formally the Representative of the Engineer, who was named in the Contract signed by the two parties (Employer and Contractor) and had the final say on all matters technical, financial and contractual. I was informed by GT on my first day that, however friendly we may be with the contractor's personnel, we must not forget our position of oversight. As visible evidence we should adhere to a dress code. We must always come to work wearing jacket and tie. If on a hot day the contractor's staff removed theirs and had open necked shirts, it was in order for us to remove our jackets, but not our ties. The rule applied only to the engineers and not the inspectors who needed to be alongside workmen, down and dirty in the excavations when required.

Jim Murphy was our measurement engineer, middle-aged and settled into middle order roles. His opposite number in Mitchells was Percy Shaw, a quantity surveyor (QS) and not an engineer – the enemy! QSs had historically had been confined to the building trade, but they were beginning to make inroads into civil engineering construction in project management roles and more particularly contractual disputes. The Conditions of Contract under which all such projects were written had, after all, been drawn up under the aegis of the Institution of Civil Engineers and the Federation of Civil Engineering Contractors – this was our territory and they were parking their tanks on our lawn.

Jim was mild-mannered and courteous, but he too was determined to maintain the upper hand, especially over a QS. In those days before the electronic calculator, computations that did not require pinpoint accuracy (when logarithmic tables would be used) were done with the aid of a slide rule. All engineers and QSs had a slide rule, but Jim was the only one I came across who had a cylindrical model, which he considered to be more accurate than the normal linear variety. If in dispute with a QS on a matter of quantity, Jim would hand the unfamiliar item to the QS and invite him to check the calculation.

Our two inspectors were quite different characters. John was small in stature, quiet and unassuming, but extremely knowledgeable and respected by the contractor, who was happy to accept his advice on the best ways of performing various tasks. Sween MacDonald was more inclined to vent his opinions without having been asked to proffer them and tended to adopt a more confrontational stance. He was a stocky and bearded highlander whose home was a croft in the north of Scotland.

At various points on the works, emergency overflows were provided, to take water away in a controlled manner if there was a failure in the control system. The overflow points were linked into a one metre diameter pipeline which led from the site, across fields, to a discharge point on the

River Kelvin about a kilometre away. Any agricultural field drains that were encountered while excavating the pipe trench had to be reinstated on completion of the work. Sween suggested to me that it would be helpful if we could identify their locations before the excavators moved in, although there was no evidence of them on the surface. “We'll have a go with dowsing, but I prefer that the contractor isn't around.” So one quiet weekend he introduced me to that black art using two lengths of fence wire bent into L shape, the shorter legs being the handles. It worked for him at that place and time, and also for me, but not something I would attempt again until many years later.

By this time Fiona and I had moved from our top floor tenement flat in Glasgow to a suburban semi-detached in Lenzie, a short commute to Balmore. So that she could get to work in the city while I went off in a different direction, I had purchased a second car, one of the first Austin Minis that had come off the production line (although early versions were badged as Sevens in homage to their iconic 1930s predecessor). It had seen better days but was a ‘runner’. The bodywork was somewhat battered, not helped when Fiona had a collision on a snowy day. I fixed that by removing the front wings and fitting a one piece fibreglass replacement comprising both wings and bonnet, the whole thing being hinged at the front such that when opened it exposed the sub frame and engine. This new front end was orange in colour and contrasted with the drab green and rust patches of the rest of the car, it remained thus for most of the period of our ownership.

An advantage of working on site was access to tradesmen and facilities. Sween taught me how to gas weld and with some scrap steel from the site I made repairs to the Mini's rusty floor wells. That done I thought I would try my hand at paint spraying. A large Nissen hut had been erected to store valuable mechanical and electrical items securely until they were needed for installation. It was spacious and there was an area where I could do the job, well away from vulnerable equipment that in any case was generally well wrapped or boxed. I wasn't especially aware of Italian cars at the time, but I was attracted by the shade ‘Positano yellow’, which transformed the look of the old Mini.

The Engineer

An oft heard gripe from UK engineers is that, unlike in many countries in Europe and elsewhere, we don't have the same protected title status as other professionals, such as medical doctors, and we are not subject to formal registration. Anyone with the minimum of qualifications can self-describe as an engineer, although not a Chartered Engineer. The problem is compounded by the failure of much of the general public to understand the distinction between a mechanic or fitter and a professionally qualified engineer with a university degree or equivalent. It was hanging offence in the office if one of the admin or other support staff, when faced with a defective copying machine, wanted to 'call out an engineer'.

An exception may however be found in the area of water storage and the provisions of the Reservoirs Act, promulgated in 1930 after disastrous reservoir failures that caused much loss of life, and updated in the current Act of 1975. Any water-containing facility such as an open reservoir or tank that (in current legislation) holds in excess of 25,000 cubic metres above the natural ground, thus risking that volume to escape suddenly in the event of failure, is required to be placed on a public register, risk assessed and subject to an annual monitoring regime.

Only civil engineers who are sufficiently qualified and experienced are permitted to certify the initial design and construction of such works, and to undertake ongoing inspections during the life of the facility. The government department which is responsible for ensuring that the legislation is adhered to maintains a register of those engineers, in four panels, all of whom must be vetted by the Reservoirs Committee of the Institution of Civil Engineers.

The reinforced concrete water storage reservoirs at Balmore fell under the provisions of that Act and senior partner, William (Bill) Cormie, OBE, was the responsible panel member. He had served with distinction in WWII as an officer in the Royal Engineers and was always immaculately dressed in his city suit. In every way he encapsulated the image and bearing of "The Engineer".

A key stage in the construction was the completion of the foundation in readiness for laying the concrete floor slabs and wall foundations. After a preliminary discussion with us in the RE's office, Cormie donned a pair of new Wellington boots and we proceeded up to the site of the raw water tank. We had been blessed with a spell of good weather and Mitchells had done an excellent job with large earth-moving equipment and dozer blades, exposing an area of smooth and levelled clay about the size of a small football pitch.

He strode about and dug his heels in a number of places, decided that there was one soft spot with which he wasn't 100% happy and instructed some remediation, but soon he declared himself otherwise quite satisfied and gave the green light. The contractor's agent was visibly relieved and immediately ordered a start to placing the 'site concrete' or 'blinding layer'. The concrete batching plant had been on standby and ready to go. It was important to get the blinding concrete laid as quickly as possible to prevent damage or softening of the exposed clay formation if there was heavy rainfall.

It was a memorable day in May of 1970 when the Queen's representative, Princess Anne, formally opened the Loch Lomond scheme. She started the pumps at Ross Priory, thus delivering the loch water through to Balmore for treatment and onward transmission eastwards. The systems had of course been thoroughly tested beforehand and it wasn't the first water to pass through the plant, but for me it signalled the end of my spell as site engineer, and with that experience behind me I was able to apply for the professional interview and reach my goal of becoming a Chartered Engineer – CEng, MICE.

4 Haiste and Partners

After finishing at the Balmore site, I returned to George Milne's Crouch and Hogg design office. It might have turned out differently had I been posted to a different department. Not that I had any issue with George or Hugh or any of my colleagues, it was a good working environment, but two years on and there were other engineers in the section of a similar or slightly higher level who had not been there when I left for Balmore, and no new graduate had been taken on. I was picking up where I left off basically and in a sense competing with the others for decent work. It was in that context that, once I passed my professional interview and became chartered, I started to look around for possible employment elsewhere. There seemed to be more opportunities in England at that time and so I attended interviews in Liverpool and Leeds.

At John H Haiste & Partners in Leeds, I was interviewed by partner Hugh Rusby Brooksbank (HRB). I felt somewhat uncomfortable with the body language from across the desk, there being short spells of silence causing me to think that my previous contribution to the discussion had been less than satisfactory, eyebrow and forehead movements being an indicator of his thoughts. It obliged one to think of something else to say and invariably one did. I came away expecting a negative result and was surprised when, a few days later, a job offer came through in the post.

Whether it was a deliberate technique of his or just his way I never really found out, others remarked upon it too and I came across it many times in his company. It was well known that fellow Yorkshireman and Prime Minister of the day, Harold Wilson, smoked a pipe which he used as a prop to give himself some thinking time. HRB didn't bother with a prop, but his thinking time was not passed idly, an honours graduate of the University of Cambridge, he had considerable intellectual capacity and the ability in a complex situation to home in on the nub of the problem and to prioritise actions.

When my resignation letter was received, Bill Cormie called me into his office. He had checked up on this firm that I intended to join and declared that, despite his being active in the upper echelons of both the Institution of Civil Engineers and the Association of Consulting Engineers, he hadn't heard either of the firm or its partners. He could not have been less impressed and tried to convince me that it was a bad move; a better future lay ahead if I stayed with them, one of the top consulting firms. I decided to stick with my decision, however, and if it didn't work out I hadn't really burned any boats, I could reasonably expect to secure a decent position either back at Crouch or with one of its competitors. I envisaged being at Haiste for a few years and then to move on again, I did not expect it to be a thirty year stint. Nearly forty years on and in the run up to retirement, I organised a company reunion. I compiled a note for that event entitled "A Haiste History", reproduced herein as an Appendix.

Our move down to Leeds on August Bank Holiday Monday of 1971 did not start well. We had had our furniture in store for a couple of weeks in a sealed container and it was waiting for us when we arrived quite early in the morning at our new house. As the movers started to take the furniture inside, Fiona cried out: "We don't have a blue carpet!" A phone call to the movers' office to inform them of their error established that our goods were about to be despatched to Inverness, but we had caught it just in time. It was not until late afternoon that our container arrived in Leeds, but in a further twist they had either forgotten the key to its padlock or had the wrong key. "Do you have a hacksaw?" I was asked. "Yes, it's in the container" I replied. Fortunately our new next door neighbour had a decent set of tools and we managed to get the doors open. Finally we were in.

Belmont House

Haiste's head office in Leeds was Belmont House, a large Edwardian villa on a quiet tree lined avenue in the pleasant suburb of Headingley. The section to which I was assigned occupied the dormer-windowed top floor of the building, which got hot in summer, requiring all of the windows and fire escape doors to be opened. Being not far from the famous rugby and cricket ground, the roars of the crowd could often be heard, which we did in August 1977 when Geoffrey Boycott scored his 100th century on home territory.

Hugh Brooksbank had only very recently merged the small family firm that was founded by his father with the much larger Haiste. He had been the sole partner, but there were two associates, Michael Dyson and Peter Roydhouse, and industrial waste specialist, Alf Sadler. In charge of the Brooksbank general design office, section leader Andrew Fountain had been promoted to that position from within Haiste. His appointment was intended to achieve rapid assimilation of Brooksbank's staff, which didn't take long in an establishment of about 60 – 70 employees.

Haiste's partners had a much more commercial outlook than their counterparts at Crouch and Hogg. Although they were members of the Association of Consulting Engineers, which had a strict code of behaviour, they pushed against the boundaries of that body's rules. Admittedly I was fairly low down the food chain at my previous employer, but I don't recall the terms 'marketing' and 'business development' ever being uttered there. Consulting engineers of the traditional type did of course promote themselves, but in a much more subtle manner.

Working for contractors on design and construct projects was very much on the agenda at Haiste, the partners were careful however not to put themselves into positions where a conflict of interest might arise when fulfilling their traditional role as independent advisers to their clients. Crouch & Hogg at that time would never have employed anyone like Haiste's Fred Firth, a snappy dresser and general man about town, the partners' right hand man when it came to seeking out commercial opportunities and doing deals. John Haiste recalls him wearing a green-hued shiny suit and winkle-picker shoes.

Always on the look-out for business opportunities, Michael Dyson had no difficulty in fitting in with the Haiste culture. From Huddersfield, he had a network of contacts in the engineering businesses of that area and they often featured in the procurement listings of various items of machinery at the sewage treatment works in our portfolio.

At Haiste there was a separate drawing office which serviced all departments. Being given a few sketches, the draughtsman produced a fully detailed engineering drawing, done in pencil onto heavyweight cartridge paper. Once the engineer had checked it over and any amendments had been made, it was then passed to a tracer who produced a version in ink on transparent film. All but one of the draughtspersons were male, but the tracers were invariably female. Most tracers were content to do just that, but a few became technical draughtswomen in their own right.

At Crouch and Hogg, projects were handled almost wholly within the individual sections, the exception to that being mechanical and electrical elements for which they had a dedicated section. Haiste also had a mechanical and electrical section, but as well as the separate drawing office there was a structural department to take care of design elements in reinforced concrete or structural steel, and a contracts department to prepare contract documents and to administer works under construction – conducting monthly measurements in conjunction with the site supervisors and issuing certificates for payments to contractors. The set up worked well, quantity surveyors were employed and within the office engineer and QS worked harmoniously. During the implementation of our projects I didn't have any hang ups about involving our chief QS in tussles of a contractual nature.

Unless the project was almost wholly of a mechanical or electrical nature, civil engineers took the lead role, it seemed to be the natural order of things. The structural and mechanical & electrical departments were pushed hard however to secure work in their own right and not be over-reliant on the workload generated by the civil departments.

Catering in the office was limited to a small kitchen where tea ladies prepared trays that they brought round to each section, morning and afternoon. At lunchtimes they made large pots of soup using tins of Campbell's condensed. In the 1970s it was quite common-place for staff to have a liquid lunch at a local pub, without regard to the reduction in work productivity that was likely to result in the afternoon. In Headingley, contingents of Haiste staff could be found either in the Skyrack or the Original Oak, the two premises facing one another on opposite sides of Otley Road. A few staff members were fairly hard drinkers, but it was tolerated provided they were perceived of as being capable of 'holding their drink' and able to turn out work of some kind afterwards. That culture died out progressively as commercial pressures enforced greater scrutiny on the outputs of sections and individuals.

Morley Sewage Works

With the exception of Starrett's Jedburgh factory, at Crouch & Hogg I had been engaged solely on water supply projects, but the clean water side of Haiste's business, once its mainstay, had shrunk, partly as a result of changes in central government spending priorities. When I joined, the bulk of the workload was concerned with sewerage and sewage treatment works.

My first project was at the sewage works for the town of Morley, to the south of Leeds. Haiste had been the Town Council's consultants, but the relationship soured and Brooksbank took it over. The council was displeased to find that, as a result of the merger, they found themselves back with Haiste. They accepted it reluctantly, on the understanding that they would deal only with Hugh Brooksbank and that none of the other Haiste partners or staff who had worked on Morley previously would be involved.

The manager at Morley Sewage Works and his deputy, Charlie Wall and John Newton respectively, were archetypical blunt Yorkshiremen, the former being sceptical of most people he had to deal with and the products or services that they provided. It was something to remark upon if a compliment came your way. An early visit to the plant was called for and duly made. It was my first time on a sewage treatment works but I knew enough about it to understand that the Morley works was atypical, employing a process that was unique to the heavy woollen district of Yorkshire, where strong grease laden waste from the scouring of wool was discharged into the public sewerage system. In reality Morley was an industrial rather than a municipal waste treatment plant.

That process, part of which entailed the heating of sludge so as to liquefy the grease fraction, produced strong odours. Lanolin was recovered from the resulting liquor and was sold for use in skin care and beauty products – I doubt very much if the purchasers of lanolin based cosmetics then knew how some of that component was sourced! Arriving home after the first day at Morley, Fiona immediately sniffed the air with displeasure and I had to strip off my clothes and have them aired or washed.

Our efforts at Morley, and at nearby Pudsey, where we were also engaged, had limited longevity. In 1974 the newly established Yorkshire Water Authority concluded that centralised treatment was preferable and proceeded to pipe the flows of waste from satellite towns into the adjacent city sewerage network, to be treated at an enlarged city works further downstream in the catchment.

Water authorities, and the privatised companies which followed, found themselves with chunks of real estate that could be developed with profit. At Morley, the site of the old works was transformed into the White Rose Centre retail complex. At Pudsey, people live in homes where once there were tanks, pumping stations and a sludge treatment centre that was one of the very few in the country to use heat rather than chemicals to condition the sludge before it was dewatered.

The reps

A typical sewage treatment works is generally more complex than a water treatment plant and the first few years at Haiste was very much a learning process for me, since there had been nothing of that kind in my undergraduate syllabus. I was at ease however in dealing with the hydraulic design aspects. The text books on sewage treatment that were published in the UK at that time were somewhat out-dated and much of what I learned was drawn from the equipment suppliers, names mostly long since gone but well known and respected then, such as Ames Crosta Mills, W E Farrar and Whitehead & Poole.

I had a bit of a soft spot for Adams Hydraulics of York. Their representative, Phil Paley, didn't go in for the hard sell, their catalogue was printed in a style that hadn't changed since the 1930s, indeed nor had many of their products, which continued to be marketed with names such as "Amphistoma" – a fascinating world of sewage ejectors, siphonic fed rotary filter distributors and the like. On a visit to the Adams foundry one took a step back in time. In later years Adams endeavoured to update their image with modern catalogues, but eventually they were bought out by a competitor. Their outgoing managing director decided that he had had enough of bearing the heavy burden of that position and found himself a job at B&Q. I was delighted to find on my internet search that the new owners have retained the Adams name and some of the original product lines live on.

The representatives of equipment and materials companies who were regular visitors to the office were generally older than me, very knowledgeable and often having been with the same employer for most of their working lives. The concept of a job for life, or at any rate a single employer for life, still prevailed in the early 1970s. An exception was the representative for a specialist pump company. Alan was my age and was as much a salesman as he was a technical representative, smart suited and go-getting. At Stressholme Sewage Treatment Works, which serves Darlington, his company obtained the order for a large twin submersible pump installation and on completion I went there to witness the testing.

We measured the output from the pumps and found it to be in line with the specification, but as the water was pulled down in the sump, the top of one pump became exposed, shortly followed by the other as the level dropped further. "The pumps aren't level" I pointed out. Quick as a flash he had the reply "No, it's not that, it's the water which is being drawn down more on one side of the well than the other and therefore it's not a level surface." Archimedes would not have been convinced and neither was I. It didn't much matter, there was nothing to be gained in re-installing one of the units to a slightly different level. In meetings with him that followed on other projects, when a suitable opportunity arose, he took my ribbing in good part.

A steady stream of representatives from various paint companies came to the office, bringing their latest by way of 'surface coating' technology ('paint' was what you bought in the DIY shop, 'surface coatings' were what you applied to steel or other construction materials to protect them from corrosion). We had a sure-fire way of dealing with them, which was to invite them to submit test pieces that we immersed in the hot and acidic liquor that came off the Morley sludge presses. Invariably they would fail after a short time in that aggressive environment, until to our surprise one passed the test. It was fortuitous as we were about to draw up a specification for a new set of settlement tank scrapers that were to be installed at the Morley works. There is only one problem they said, a bit like Henry Ford's model T, you can have it in any colour provided it's black. It was more usual to finish these machines in a blue or green shade, but it transpired that they were able to formulate it in a dark brown and we settled for that.

1974

For most consulting civil engineers, the bulk of fee income derives from the planning, design and execution of infrastructure. In 1974, well before the idea of privatisation of services had entered the political realm, Haiste's main client base comprised municipalities ranging from small urban and rural district councils to city and county authorities. A central government review concluded that this was not an efficient way to provide services at a local level and a comprehensive reorganisation took place in which urban and rural district councils were abolished, city councils were expanded, and a number of new metropolitan councils were created. The majority of Haiste's clients were disbanded and what had hitherto been a reasonably secure and steady income stream dried up.

Further compounding the upheaval was the formation of brand new water and sewerage authorities, those functions having been taken away from local government. It was the bulk of our business and suddenly we had to make new relationships with the successor bodies, which, being larger entities than their predecessors, were forming new capital works departments with in-house capabilities. They saw less need for external consultants.

A great deal of empire building went on. In the rationalisation, municipal employees who didn't find a comparable post in the new authority were ousted comfortably with generous pay-offs and pension packages. By contrast, engineers employed by private firms whose survival was under threat were made redundant and had to leave with the modest statutory minimum. It was a disaster for many consulting engineering firms all over the country and an unequal outcome for engineers working in the private and public sectors.

One of the council clients for whom Haiste had worked for many years presented the firm with a plaque in recognition of the long service that had been given and which the councillors acknowledged had been of benefit to their community. It was appreciatively received, but it marked the end of an era.

Whether the Haiste partners had the foresight to see this coming, or had in any case decided that in their continuing search for new business they should look overseas for it, I do not know, perhaps it was a combination of both. But it saved the firm and enabled it to survive when others didn't.

5 Iraq

At a time when ancient Britons were seemingly eking out a primitive tribal existence, civilisation was being cradled elsewhere, including in the lands of ancient Mesopotamia, which means literally the land between two rivers (the Tigris and the Euphrates).

For civilisation to take root and flourish, arguably the rule of law and due process is fundamental. From 1792 to 1750 BC, Babylon was ruled by Hammurabi, who established 282 laws that included economic provisions such as those governing prices, tariffs, trade and commerce, as well as family, criminal and civil laws. Of relevance to civil engineers and touching on a later chapter in this book, I quote from the translation by L W King:

> *229: If a builder builds a house for someone and does not construct it properly, and the house falls and kills its owner, then that builder shall be put to death.*
>
> *230: If it kills the son of the owner, the son of the builder shall be put to death.*
>
> *232. If it ruins goods, he shall make compensation for all that has been ruined, and inasmuch as he did not construct properly this house which he built and it fell, he shall re-erect the house at his own expense.*

Law 232 fits comfortably with today's legislation. The punishment provisions of Laws 229 and 230 would not be seen in any civilised country today and one can feel only sympathy for the son of a builder.

The modern state of Iraq did not come into being until 1917, following the defeat of the Ottoman empire. For around four hundred years, Turks had ruled over the whole of that territory as well as what is now Kuwait and the United Arab Emirates. Under the Sykes-Picot agreement between Britain and France, Britain took control of Iraq and established a monarchy under King Faisal the First. Independence followed in 1932, but Britain retained military bases there and intervened again to exercise control after Iraq sided with Germany during World War II. In 1958 the state became a republic, in a bloody coup that involved mutilated regal body parts being dragged through the streets. The Ba'ath party came to power in 1963, its reign finally coming to an end with the invasion of America, Britain and other allies in the second Gulf War of 2003.

Between 1972 and 1980, the price of crude oil rose almost fivefold in real (inflation adjusted) terms[9], triggered by an embargo on the sale of oil to western countries imposed by the Organization of Arab Petroleum Exporting Countries (OPEC). This was their response to the United States' support for Israel during the 1973 'Yom Kippur' war. The bulk of the national income of the oil rich states in the Middle East was derived from the black crude. With such new wealth at their disposal, the states' rulers were in a position both to enrich themselves and their families and still have plenty left over to spend massively on public works projects and on welfare for their populations. It ushered in a golden era for civil engineers and others working in the built environment, for those prepared to do so in countries with radically different social and cultural norms to their home nations[10].

Back in the 1930s, in circumstances which no one in the office seemed to know, Haiste had been responsible for a floating pontoon bridge in Kenya. Invariably it was quoted in promotional literature to show that the firm had been active overseas for a considerable period of time. We had a grainy black and white photograph to prove it. In the 1960s and early 70s there were some ventures in Nigeria and in Italy and Spain, but they were relatively modest in scope. There were rich pickings to be had in the Gulf states – Saudi Arabia and the Emirates – many of the big names in UK consultancy were well entrenched there. Haiste managed to establish a small operation in Saudi Arabia, but despite a number of attempts the firm failed to gain any work in Dubai, Kuwait or the UAE. It had more success however in Iran (before the revolution), Iraq and Libya. Iraq and Libya were seen as more difficult markets and the competition for work less intense.

In 1975, Hugh Brooksbank secured Haiste's first commission in Iraq, a sewerage scheme for the city of Ramadi, some 120 km to the west of

Baghdad. I was to be the senior engineer and preparations were made for me to travel out there in rapid order, only a few short weeks after the birth of my son, Neil. If I had any reservations about it I suppressed them, I went along with it on the basis that I couldn't let the firm down and I would give it my best; if I didn't take to it I would be looking for another job.

In the years that followed there were to be countless tussles with bureaucratic procedures that, if they had parallels in the UK, would have been straightforward to deal with, but elsewhere they could often take up inordinate amounts of time and effort, documentation to be certified and stamped and notarised and translated, involving the employment of persons who were on officially recognised registers. And so it went on.

The application for my Iraqi visa required a copy of my baptism certificate, a document which up to that time I hadn't needed and wasn't aware that it didn't exist. We were regular church goers, as pretty much everyone was in the 1940s and 50s, but my father explained to me that it was wartime when I was born and my parents had just not got round to having me baptised, there being much else going on at the time. After WWII was over my sister was born and she was baptised, but this was a procedure that applied to babies they felt and not to four year olds, so that was that.

Underlying the Iraqis' requirement for a certificate of baptism was the bar on anyone of the Jewish faith, of which there are significant numbers living in Leeds. One of my colleagues in the office did come from a Jewish family, albeit he was 'non-practising', so there was no chance that he would be despatched to Iraq. It was of no account that Baghdad had been a Jewish settlement before it became a predominantly Muslim city. According to Marozzi[11], in the early 20th century there were still some 40,000 Jewish inhabitants, the evidence for which I saw for myself in the form of stars of David on buildings which had been synagogues or otherwise Jewish owned. But in revolutionary Iraq the ruling Ba'ath party adopted a hostile stance towards Israel and Zionism.

I came up with the solution of making a formal sworn and signed statement, declaring that I had been brought up as a Christian by Christian parents, I had never visited Israel and had no intention of doing so. The Iraq embassy rejected it. The brother of an associate of the firm was a vicar in the Church of England; no matter that I had been Church of Scotland, subject to him being satisfied as to my origins and character he was prepared to provide a document on C of E headed note paper, declaring that I was of the Christian faith. I went to see him at his parish church in Burley-in-Wharfedale, a small town between Leeds and Ilkley. I felt a bit embarrassed about it, but the Reverend Donald Aldred, brother of Ian, was used to helping his parishioners with all manner of requests and he put me at my ease. He issued the requested document promptly and it secured my Iraqi visa.

Communications

It will be difficult for the current generation to imagine a world without instantaneous communications by 'phone and email across continents and into the most remote of regions. In travelling out to Iraq for the first time, contact with back home involved sparing use of the public telex facility. One was conveniently situated adjacent to the Baghdad Hotel, where we stayed during the first missions, in the heart of the central business district, just off the main thoroughfare, Sadoun Street. Like an extended telegram, one completed a form with the message spelled out in capital letters and queued up at the telex office where it would be checked and sent. Nothing of an intimate or commercially sensitive nature could be conveyed by that means. It was possible to make a telephone call, but that had to be booked well in advance and one would be given an approximate time slot that wasn't always honoured. It went without saying that all calls were monitored by state security.

Eventually telex machines were permitted in private offices under strict licence, it was hugely beneficial. Telephoning was still difficult, but it was possible to hold a two way conversation on the telex, a bit like the modern SMS. There was a bell key which could be pressed at the end of one's message, alerting the operator or colleague at the other end that you had finished but that you were remaining on line, ready to receive a reply. In the private office of our Iraqi representative, the telex machine in the corner was a great comforter. 557131 HAISTE G was the Leeds office telex address.

It was generally believed that the drivers of the mechanically reliable and internally clean taxis that were available from the rank outside the Baghdad Hotel were paid to report on the conversations of foreigners and therefore, while a passenger, one should confine oneself to inconsequential chit-chat. Similarly, any criticism of conditions found or of the regime or any of its agencies should not be expressed in the back of a cab.

The sense of being far from home was heightened by the journey from Leeds to Baghdad. A British Midland Vickers Viscount turbo-prop aircraft, with its large oval windows offering a good view out, flew us down to London Heathrow. There was then a flight out to Beirut, either by British Airways (BA) or by Middle East Airlines (MEA), the Lebanese national airline. The final leg into Baghdad was either by MEA or Iraqi Airways. In later years Iraqi Airways flew directly between Heathrow and Baghdad, as did British Airways who flew Vickers VC10s, smooth and quiet rear-engined 'planes that passengers generally preferred to Boeings, but which fell out of favour with airlines due to their heavier fuel consumption.

At the end of a mission, having endured the rigours of getting through Baghdad airport and the thorough exit border checks, it was a relief to board the 'plane for home. BA's cabin service on the return journey seemed to be especially attentive, even in economy class. At the earliest opportunity a steward came round and took the drinks orders, to be served to you as soon as cruising height was reached, no long wait while a drinks trolley made its slow way along the aisle. A system of coloured pennants pinned into the top of the seat headrest was used, to denote the order and facilitate rapid delivery of one's gin and tonic or whatever.

On returning home after my first visit to Baghdad I realised that I had not had a single asthmatic attack, an affliction that was a regular occurrence especially if I had to sleep in a strange bed, this being a good many years before the development of anti-inflammatory steroid based inhalers that could give relief. I put it down to the hot dry climate. During the following eight years, while travelling around Iraq and on visits to other countries in the Middle East, I was generally in better health there than I was back at home in the UK.

We had business cards printed with Arabic text on the reverse. Other companies did the same but one had made a rather basic error, with the

Arabic having been printed left to right and not right to left. On presenting his card for the first time, the unfortunate company rep had been met with a puzzled look followed by laughter. Holding it up to a mirror the official was able to read it, although he would not have had any difficulty with the English on the reverse. Not an ideal start to try to impress a potential new client!

Al Khazen

Our local partner for the Ramadi project, and the Four Cities schemes which followed, was consulting engineer Al-Khazen. It was a one man band basically, but that one man, Dr Ali, had formidable presence and exuded power and control by posture, gesture and gaze. Originally from Mosul in the north of Iraq, he had held the position of Minister of Planning at one time, so he moved in high circles.

Al-Khazen's office was on the second floor of an office block at the junction of Sadoun and Jumhouriya Streets, overlooking Tahrir (Liberation) Square. Despite its city centre location, the common areas of the building were rather grubby. Tahrir square is notable for its huge mural, in bronze relief mounted on a marble frieze, erected to commemorate the establishment of the Republic of Iraq after the bloody overthrow of the royal family. The mural depicts a number of scenes from Iraq's history going back to the ancient Sumerians. The presence of a circular object resembling a ball meant that the junction was known universally to expatriate Brits as 'Spot the Ball Square' (Spot the Ball being a popular competition within the sporting pages of newspapers of the day).

There were no women in the Al Khazen office. The secretary / typist was an efficient and competent man who spoke good English. He was respectful of Dr Ali but not in any way subservient, I took that to be on account of his Assyrian origin of which he was proud. By contrast, Dr Ali's no. 2, Bashir, was a nervy individual in awe of his boss. Those nerves were no less evident when driving around in his old Soviet Volga car in which, while peering through spectacles of dubious prescription, he piloted his way through the Baghdad traffic with sudden changes of direction and speed, in a succession of lurches, either accelerating or braking but rarely proceeding at a steady pace.

After a working session in the evening – the working day was divided with a long lunch and rest break in the hottest part of the day – Dr Ali sometimes took us to dinner at one of his favourite restaurants. He would drive us there in his Mercedes-Benz, a mid range model in Europe, common enough in Germany as a taxi, but in Baghdad a car that was generally the preserve of senior government officials and party members. As soon as we entered, Dr Ali would be recognised and the proprietor or head waiter would come across smartly to receive us personally. In full deferential mode he would show us to a table, enquiring first if it was suitable for us, since if not he would arrange a different one.

There was a little ritual when a basket of flat breads was brought for us to nibble with a few olives or other crudités, while we decided on and waited for our food. Dr Ali would gently place the back of his hand onto the top of the stack of bread, to check that it was fresh and warm, if not the waiter would be summoned and it had to be taken away and replaced quickly with bread of acceptable standard.

Azzouz

It was difficult to conduct business in Iraq, or indeed anywhere else in the Middle East, without being represented by a local resident who knew the ropes and had connections. Traditional agents who worked on a sales commission basis were banned in Iraq, ostensibly to stop such commissions simply being used as a front for bribes to those in a position to place orders and enter into commercial contracts. However it was in order to be a "representative" who for a fee provided services to a foreign firm or firms. Such services did not exclude facilitating introductions to potential clients, but could include the provision of office accommodation, local communications and transport, etc.

We were represented by Hanna Azzouz, a cultured gentleman from a wealthy and well connected family, those connections dating back to before the revolution. There must have been sufficient distance between the Azzouz and royal families for the former not to have been ostracised or worse when the latter were ousted in bloody fashion.

Hanna was always immaculately turned out, courtesy of his London tailor and gentleman's outfitter. Only in visits to his home did I see him without a jacket and tie. Home in Baghdad was a fine house in Mansour, the Kensington and Chelsea of Iraq's capital city. His second home was an apartment in Dolphin Square, London SW1.

Hanna was an anglophile. As well as Haiste, he also represented Braithwaite, manufacturers of prefabricated steel panel water storage tanks, and Stanton & Staveley (subsequently British Steel), makers of cast and ductile iron pipes for water supply and sewage pressure mains. He represented British Airways too and that connection came in useful to us from time to time.

Hanna's small office on Sadoun Street was in the centre of the main commercial district, opposite the Baghdad Hotel and the public telex office. Looking after the day to day running of the office was his main assistant, Jousef Haddad, somewhat crumpled in dress and demeanour but unfailingly helpful. A vital member of the team was a slightly built gentleman in his 60s, always in a black suit with clean white shirt and dark tie, he occupied the small kitchen and cleaning room. He kept the office spick and span and produced refreshments on demand. As in most offices, the standard drink was sweetened black tea in small glasses, but for a special treat he would make 'hamouth' tea, made with dried lemons. He knew that I had a great liking for it and on my visits he made a point of stocking up on the core ingredient.

In the UK I have two particular memories of Hanna. He had come to our Leeds office for meetings there and his visit coincided with the British general election in 1979. I invited him for dinner at my home to join us and to watch the election coverage on TV. I discovered that my drinks cupboard was devoid of whisky and knowing that Hanna, like many Arabs, appreciated a 'Scotch on the rocks', Fiona made a rapid trip to our local pub where she worked part time behind the bar. The bottle thus obtained sustained us through the night and into the early hours of the next morning, both of us glued to the TV screen as the results came in, the swingometer swung and the Thatcher era began. It saddened him that his home country was ruled by a dictator and did not enjoy the parliamentary democracy and freedoms that we take for granted.

Many years later, as the millennium approached and more than a decade after I had stopped visiting Iraq, he got in touch and invited me for a meal in London where he was then living. We reminisced over those times and he revealed to me that, while he represented us in Iraq, he was reporting on our activities to the state security department. It wasn't that they made him an offer he couldn't refuse, it was one that he daren't refuse if he valued his life and livelihood. He explained to me that he tried his best to feed them intelligence that was innocent and unlikely to be useful or harmful to our interests if known.

As far as I was aware we conducted our affairs in a straight and ethical manner and we should have had nothing to fear in that respect, but I confess to considerable ignorance of what kind of intelligence, however innocent, could be useful to the agencies of dictators like Saddam Hussein. It wouldn't have been difficult to be drawn into the world of 'backsheesh', and, like the unfortunate Ian Richter from the UK water treatment company, Paterson Candy, find oneself incarcerated for years in the notorious Abu Ghraib prison.

Ramadi and the Four Cities

I recall making only the one visit to our first project in Iraq, Ramadi, which lies on the left bank of the River Euphrates. To gain some rapid familiarity with the layout of the city and to identify potential sites for the sewage treatment works and surface water drainage pumping stations, we were taken around by the municipality's chief engineer and his young assistant who spoke good English. There was a reasonable set of plans and examining an Iraqi survey plan for the first time I enquired of the young engineer about a plot of land that was shown with crescent motifs. "That's where the dead people live" he explained. I understood immediately.

In terms of its scope, the Four Cities project was a repeat of Ramadi, requiring us to produce feasibility studies, designs and contract documents for works of sewerage and sewage treatment for the southern cities of Hilla, Diwaniyah and Samawah, on the River Euphrates, and for Kut on the River Tigris. By this time we had bottomed many of the unknowns with which we were presented at Ramadi, such as rainfall intensity data, per capita water consumption and pollution loads.

A considerable benefit of working overseas is the opportunity to visit places somewhat off the beaten track that one would be fairly unlikely to go otherwise, but with someone else, namely one's employer, picking up the bill. In the 1970s tourism hardly figured at all as an economic activity in Iraq, despite it having a fantastically rich heritage. Tragically the country has now descended into sectarian violence and strife, so the prospect of developing a tourist industry is more remote than ever.

I count myself fortunate to have been able to visit and stroll safely around the remains of the Hanging Gardens of Babylon, which are on the outskirts of the modern city of Hilla. President Saddam Hussein saw himself as the successor to King Nebuchadnezzar and embarked on a reconstruction and reproduction of the original, a procedure which I imagine modern Western archaeologists would frown upon. Arguably there were precedents, however, such as the palace of Knossos on Crete which was partly reconstructed in the 1900s by British archaeologist Sir Arthur Evans. At around the same time as Evans was making his discoveries at Knossos, German archaeologist Robert Koldewey was engaged in a similar endeavour at Babylon where he uncovered the remains of the splendid Ishtar Gate. But instead of reconstructing it in situ, as Evans did at Knossos, the remains of the gate were removed from the site and taken to Berlin.

Some twenty years after visiting Babylon I was in the Pergamon Museum in Berlin, unaware of the connection. Through an archway I wandered into the ancient Mesopotamian room and it was a déjà vu moment when I realised that I was about to emerge through the Ishtar Gate, except that this time I was seeing fragments of the original brightly coloured glazed bricks, that had been pieced together in an impressive reconstruction of the two and a half thousand year old edifice.

Saddam Hussein's reproduction was damaged during the 2003 Iraq war, so whatever one might think of the expropriation of Iraq's ancient artefacts by western archaeologists at a time when there was no indigenous authority able to prevent it, those actions saved them from the further degradation that would have occurred in the course of modern conflict.

On my first visit to Hilla, after our initial reconnaissance around the city, we returned to the city engineer's office where glasses of chilled water awaited us. They had a rather cloudy appearance and I looked askance, but he assured us that it was 'good Hilla water'. Cloudiness *per se* is not a problem, sometimes caused by inaccurate dosing and carry-over of coagulant from the water treatment plant, but not long afterwards my internal workings signalled to me in unambiguous terms that the cloudy water was also home to some less than friendly bacteriological life.

The city of Kut is the site of a tragic episode of World War I, when in 1916 an 8,000 strong British-Indian garrison was besieged by the Ottoman Army and was forced to surrender after many had perished. The survivors were then marched to imprisonment at Aleppo in Syria, where many more died. When we visited in 1976 in the course of our local fact-finding, we found the cemetery where the graves of the British war dead are interred to be quite well tended. As soon as we turned up, the person responsible for looking after it appeared and welcomed us warmly, he earned a stipend from the Commonwealth War Graves Commission. Despite the ongoing hostilities in the country, in 2014 the Commission managed to have it completely renovated ahead of the centenary of the incident[12].

The southernmost and smallest of the four cities was Samawah. The available survey plans were of poorer quality than at the other cities and we had them spread out on a large table, I was trying to find my bearings so I asked the city's engineer to show me where on the plans we were now, in his office. That was a difficult question for him and it took some time in discussion with colleagues before he was able to pinpoint it.

Samawah had a busy souk with a thriving metal wares section and I watched impressed as a coppersmith made a beautifully shaped and proportioned water carrier out of a flat sheet of the material. Once the basic shape had been roughly formed on his bench, he sat on the ground with legs stretched out and used his feet and knees to hold the vessel in position and rotate it as if it was on a mandrel, whilst beating it into final shape and giving it a decorative hammered pattern. I choose one of the smaller ones that I hoped I could take home on the 'plane, either in the hold or as cabin baggage. He was reluctant to let me have it as it hadn't yet been lined with pitch to make it waterproof, but as I was leaving town in a few hours and intended it for decorative use that didn't matter. To him it was simply an everyday practical object. To me it was an artefact of beauty, an example of the traditional skills that had been deployed in the region for many hundreds of years.

Travelling south to the four cities from Baghdad involved a very early start, so that we reached our destination and completed as much outdoor fact-finding as possible before the heat of the sun reached maximum intensity. Dr Ali had air conditioning in his Mercedes, but for our journeys he provided a large American car with bench seats and non sweat absorptive clear plastic covers, lacking the facility of passenger compartment cooling that he enjoyed himself. As a compensatory feature the boot contained a large cool box filled with ice and cold drinks.

The regular driver that Dr Ali employed was competent and reliable, but even he was caught out sometimes by the random nature of the temporary road signs employed at the stretches of road works under way in upgrading the main Baghdad to Basra highway. On one occasion we were returning to Baghdad in the evening and he had followed the temporary signs that directed us onto a section of the new carriageway, or so the driver thought. We were half asleep in the back seat when suddenly the car came to a tyre smoking and swerving halt, just short of a near precipice at the unmarked temporary termination of that bit of road construction, on a 3m high embankment as it approached a partly completed bridge.

I became acclimatised to working in the hot dry climate in Iraq and felt I could cope even on the hottest of days, perhaps becoming rather blasé, until a visit to the Samawah cement factory. I was there in connection with our sewerage project and Dr Ali had arranged for me to be put up overnight at the factory's guest house. The cement factory had been one of Al Khazen's projects and he asked if I could assist him by making an inspection of a certain part of the plant, which was in operation. It required me to get close to the cement kiln and in the afternoon sun the heat was intense. With my notes in hand I only just managed to stagger back to the guest house where, feeling nauseous, I collapsed onto the bed, drank as much water as I could and was then out for the count for more than 12 hours.

Sewer and Treatment Works Designs

In 1960s Iraq, only a few urban centres, such as parts of Baghdad on the east bank of the river and some self-contained individual developments, had piped sewerage systems and treatment of the waste before discharge.

In the1970s 'our' cities and several others received funding to provide these facilities. It was a given that Iraq, in common with other oil rich states, would want sanitation solutions that were not seen in any way inferior to the norm in western Europe. Anything different that may well have been more suited to the local situation was not looked upon with any favour, being regarded as appropriate only for third world countries. In the face of client reluctance we did not dwell on these alternatives.

To some extent we did break from convention when it came to sewage treatment. For any town of, say, 50,000 population and above, it was usual in that era to adopt as the basic treatment process either what is termed conventional aeration, or trickling biological filters, in both cases preceded by a primary settlement stage. The resulting solid matter from both primary and secondary settlement is typically treated by anaerobic digestion, a complex process that demands skilled operation. Notwithstanding that our cities ranged in size from 120,000 to 350,000, we were not convinced that the resources to run such plants effectively would be forthcoming and so we were reluctant to recommend those processes.

For smaller plants a much simpler process known as extended aeration had been growing in popularity, albeit with the disadvantage that it entailed significantly greater electrical power consumption. But given that Iraq was a country sitting on huge reserves of energy – we had another project at the time in partnership with the General Electric Company to install small modular power stations throughout Iraq – our client accepted our recommendation to adopt extended aeration for Ramadi and the Four Cities. In another innovation, to simplify construction we designed the large aeration tanks in the form of concrete lined earth embankment basins.

Production of the several volumes of contract documents in many copies remained reliant on technology that pre-dated the Rank Xerox photocopier. We were still in the carbon paper age. For a large and professional print job one could use an outside printer, and printing was a major industry in Leeds so that was readily to hand if we so chose, but for the sizes of print runs that we had, offices like ours normally utilised a Gestetner or Roneo duplicating machine.

Originals were typed onto what were known as 'skins', flimsy material that was punctured through with the typewriter key, the inked typewriter ribbon that normally produced printed characters onto a paper page having been removed. There was limited scope for correcting typing or compositional errors. Small alterations of a few characters could be made using a red repair fluid, but anything more, like adding a sentence, required the whole page to be retyped, and might also affect the following page.

The method was not popular with secretarial staff, but in Ellen Mackie who worked in our contracts department we had a great asset, as she could type page after page with barely an error. Providing a legible draft was of vital importance, much of it comprising physical cut and paste from previous documents, annotated and supplemented with new handwritten text. Ellen could draw on many years of experience, she knew a wide range of technical and contractual words and phrases, she understood what she was typing and would check with you if she thought it may not be correct.

Samarra Water Supply

With Ramadi and the Four Cities in progress, our relationship with the State Organisation for Water and Sewerage Projects (SOWASP) seemed to be progressing satisfactorily and we were awarded the job of designing a scheme to augment the water supply to the town of Samarra, situated on the River Tigris 140 km north west of Baghdad. It wasn't a complex project – the enlargement of the existing raw water pumping station and treatment plant, and extensions to the town's distribution network. To design the network of distribution pipes we used a computer model for the first time. The UK's Water Research Centre had devised a very basic programme, 'NETMODS', which was to become the forerunner to considerable advances made in that area in the years following. At that time we relied on external computer support to perform the number-crunching.

I was rather pleased with the results of our efforts and turned up at the office of SOWASP's project manager expecting a positive reception. In the Middle East, someone in a senior position has a large office, not only reflecting his or her status, but enabling several meetings to be conducted concurrently. Traditional hospitality demands that when you arrive you are offered some refreshment and the time to unwind and recover from your journey before getting down to the business in hand. While you are doing this, the meeting that was already under way when you came in continues. On a busy day an executive may have several encounters running in parallel.

On this occasion my arrival coincided with a meeting between our client and an engineer from one of our competitors, Irish consultants Jennings O'Donovan. After we had taken our ease with the sweet tea, and apparently not having finished his business with Jennings' man, the project manager turned to me and I found myself on the receiving end of a 'good telling off', something in the documents we had sent for his review clearly displeased him. My Irish competitor sat across the room taking it all in with a smug look on his face at my embarrassment.

Sometimes you know that the quality of what you have turned out is not of the standard to which you might aspire, but this was not one of those, so his outburst was unexpected. In such situations one has to decide quickly whether to defend robustly and fight fire with fire or to concede whilst seeking mitigation of some kind. On the basis of the customer always being right I took the latter course of action and since eventually we did get paid it couldn't have been too bad.

Najaf-Kufa

As the 1970s progressed, projects for which funding became available in the early-mid part of the decade, allowing planning and designs to be prepared, reached the stage of physical realisation, as contracts for construction were tendered and then awarded. Authorities like SOWASP were then faced with the task of supervising the appointed contractors. It was obvious that they could not muster the resources required from inside the country and that resulted in a further wave of commissions for consulting engineers to provide site supervision and general contract management services.

The model that was generally adopted was to appoint an Iraqi engineer as the official site supervisor (Resident Engineer) who had powers of technical, financial and contractual oversight, assisted by expatriate Contract Advisers provided by consultants such as ourselves. The Contract Advisers did not have any formal authority over the contractors, but they were on hand to support the Iraqi engineers, many of whom were young and inexperienced. How the model worked out depended very much on the personal working relationship between Resident Engineer and Adviser(s).

Our first such commission was the supervision of the Najaf-Kufa Sewerage Scheme, twin cities some 150 km south of Baghdad and revered holy sites to Shia Muslims. Two of Iraq's five golden domed mosques are at Najaf and Kufa, the others being in Baghdad, Samarra and Kerbala. Imam Ali, son-in-law of the prophet Muhammad and regarded by Shiites as his true heir, reportedly is buried at the Najaf shrine. The construction contract had been awarded to an Indian company, Bridge and Roof.

Our contract provided for senior and assistant Contract Advisers to be resident on site, with head office technical and administrative back-up that was delivered mainly by periodic visits from a partner or other senior engineer. The senior site position was filled initially by Stuart Ashton, who we recruited specifically for the project, he had previous experience working in the Middle East. A few years later Trevor Moore, a Haiste employee of several years standing, took over when Stuart left. The assistant's post was taken by John Falkingham, who had relevant UK experience but at the time none overseas, he joined us from Yorkshire Water Authority but he had been with Haiste as a graduate engineer.

Stuart and John were our first resident personnel in the country, they had to become registered with the authorities, arrange housing and furnishing thereof, open bank accounts etc. Cars had to be imported from Kuwait and were subject to different regulations and tax regimes from those owned by locals, being readily identifiable by their blue number plates. By this time fortunately we had local representation, Azzouz, who were vital in helping our staff negotiate the bureaucratic maze. Whether any 'baksheesh' was involved we didn't know or wish to know.

The Najaf-Kufa sewage treatment works had been designed by a French consultant and was based on the trickling biological filtration system. Instead of large tanks containing the waste, with mechanical aeration to create the oxygen-rich conditions for helpful bacteria to thrive, this low energy method relies upon a different breed of bacterium which lives, not within a basin of liquid, but as a slime on the surfaces of millions of pieces of stone within filter 'beds' through which the settled waste trickles.

Quarried stone had to be broken down and sieved into the specified sizes. Normally this would be done using mechanical crushing and grading machinery, but an image of visits to the works that sticks in my mind is of seeing two Indian labourers sitting cross-legged at the foot of a huge pile of freshly quarried stone, manually breaking up the larger pieces into the smaller sizes required by the specification, using hammers and chisels. On successive visits several weeks apart I was only just able to detect a modest transfer of material from the one heap to the other, but they had time on their side as it would take many months of site construction before the tanks were ready to receive the filter media.

It was truly hard labour as practised in prisons in various jurisdictions and I suspect that it would have been of little comfort to the unfortunate labourers to know that a future winner of the Nobel Peace prize, Nelson Mandela, was obliged by his jailors to perform the same task on Robben Island. I thought of those Indians when I visited the former South African equivalent of Alcatraz in the 2000s, by then a popular tourist attraction.

Kerbala

Not far from Najaf-Kufa is another Shia holy city, Kerbala. There we had to provide only a senior adviser and Larry Brindle was our man, supervising the construction of a sewerage scheme that had been designed by Danish consultants, Cowi.

Whereas Stuart and John were unmarried and living in Iraq as bachelors, Larry was married with a daughter and once settled in a house in Kerbala he planned to bring his family out. He explained to us that Liz was extremely fastidious in relation to household cleanliness and we worried that it might all end in tears, these towns were dusty places and left a bit to be desired in respect of garbage collection and street cleaning. Larry had given the rented house a thorough clean before she arrived, but it left what one might describe as tertiary levels of historic and more stubborn grime. Liz tackled it with enthusiasm – a cocktail stick was her tool of choice for dealing with deposits in the interstices and screw heads of light switches.

Hilla and Diwaniyah

At Hilla and Diwaniyah, our senior advisers were Ivor Wayne and Steve respectively, chalk and cheese in a sense. Ivor had been employed by us as a resident engineer in the UK and was of the 'old school gentleman' type. Steve was a tough former contractor's agent whose former boss at Galliford Construction I had crossed swords with on a job in Sleaford in Lincolnshire. Together with Stuart, John and Larry, they comprised a group of engineers who were mutually supportive of one another in our southern provincial sphere of operations and had a 'can do' attitude to the jobs in hand. We had a small budget on each job for head office back up and it is a testament to the abilities and performance of those colleagues that it proved to be adequate.

Like Bridge & Roof at Najaf, the contractor for both Hilla and Diwaniyah was also from India, although Continental Construction was a larger enterprise. After the site inspections and progress meetings, it was one of the pleasures of my trips there to accept their hospitality at the manager's residence, where his Indian cook had prepared a fine meal. The delights of that cuisine passed Steve by however and he would invariably be served with steak and chips, over which he sprinkled liberal quantities of salt and pepper.

I do not recall Steve eating anything else, although I suppose he must have done. Whether it was his diet that took its toll I cannot say, but a few years later, after he had left our employment, I received a telephone call from his wife, seeking our assistance. He had gone on to obtain a post in Saudi Arabia where he was employed by a local rather than a UK company, he had died suddenly out in that country and his now widow was struggling to deal with the formalities. She knew that we had an office in Saudi and I readily agreed to contact my colleagues there to do what they were able to assist with local enquiries and administrative procedures.

Project 8505

For some reason the relationship that we had with Dr Ali and Al Khazen, that had got us started in Iraq, ran out of steam; there was no falling out, just no more joint opportunities in the pipeline. With Dr Ali's acquiescence we entered into collaboration with another small consultancy, Philip Nacy, one of whose clients was the Ministry of Defence, an organisation with a very large estate. We obtained a commission to design a scheme of sewerage and sewage treatment for a large army camp outside the city of Baqubah, the capital of Iraq's Diyala Governorate, some 50 km to the northeast of Baghdad.

The job was not difficult technically, but there were security considerations associated with our appointment. One of those was that none of the documents or drawings should give any indication of where the project was located or of the nature of the establishment. This led to a debate with the client on what the project would be titled. The Ministry's procurement officer concluded that it was best not to give it a local name of any kind since some bright 'spy' might follow the same train of thought and discover it. The job numbers for Iraq in our office were all of the 8000 series and as it was 8505 in our office, the Ministry were happy to adopt that as the title of the project.

Construction got under way around 1979 or 1980, the appointed contractor being managed and supervised by military personnel, equivalent to our Royal Engineers. We provided technical back up during construction and this mainly took the form of one of our engineers attending periodic site meetings with the contractor and the military supervisors. After the start of the Iraq-Iran war, in September 1980, those visits were made with some caution as the camp lay only 70 km or so from the Iranian border to the east. However construction continued, albeit slowly, and there were still technical issues to be resolved.

By this stage we had a growing team of expatriate personnel in Baghdad and our senior design engineer, John Haiste, went to the site meetings. He recalls: "Security was amazingly slack, I could just drive into the camp with a cursory glance, past captured Iranian tanks (British made Chieftains). Once I saw a batch of Yemeni boy soldiers with guns (looked about 12 years old) sitting on bags of kit, waiting to be transported to the front."

Despite the conflict that was going on beyond its perimeter, work on the camp's infrastructure did not suffer from lack of oversight, as John Haiste attests: "There were about 25 engineering officers from 2nd Lieutenant through to Brigadier. After an inconclusive meeting of at least two hours conducted entirely in Arabic, I was asked to write yet another report on whether it was necessary to incorporate waterstops in construction joints in manholes."

6 Baghdad

Baghdad Sewer Relining

Having got us established in Iraq, Hugh Brooksbank then transferred his energies to bolster the efforts being made by another partner, Harvey Roberts, to achieve a similar presence for the firm in Libya, or to give it its full name: the Socialist Peoples' Libyan Arab Jumhuria, SPLAJ for short. Hugh's successor as partner in charge for Iraq was Bernard Eagles, who then became my boss and with whom I worked closely and harmoniously for the next five years.

Hugh had already been knocking on the door of the Baghdad Sewerage Board (BSB) and we learned that they were greatly concerned with the growing problem of internal corrosion of their sewers which, when the corrosion reached a critical level, the sewer pipe would collapse in a structural failure. Various remedial solutions had been tried in conjunction with their then long-serving consultant, John Taylor & Sons, but with not much success.

If we had been in Taylor's position I expect we would have gone down a similar route, but the BSB were by then receptive to ideas coming from other sources. We were awarded a commission to study the corrosion problem in more detail and to come up with a permanent solution for the existing trunk sewer that connected the city to Rustamiyah sewage treatment works on the east bank of the River Tigris. Collapse of a subsidiary sewer in a suburban street was disruptive enough, but for it to happen to the trunk sewer would have been a public health and environmental disaster, not to mention the repercussions from on high for the directors of the Board.

The problem was endemic throughout the Middle East. Without going into the biochemistry, suffice it to say that *thiobacillus concretivorus* was the villain of the piece. With my colleague Ian Aldred, we had to make an internal inspection of the existing 2.3m diameter trunk sewer in a number of places, a potentially dangerous exercise. He was senior to me and bravely volunteered to do most of it, while I watched over the BSB's surface crew who were manning the pump that delivered fresh air to him down a flexible hose tube. It was a hand-cranked device and I was ready to step in and take over if the BSB operative showed any sign of easing up. His life was in our hands.

Manhole covers had been removed upstream and downstream of the inspection location and a large electrically driven air pump delivered a stream of fresh air through the sewer. At one point the supply of direct air to Ian's face mask started to fail, despite the hand pump being continuously operated. Ian had no alternative but to remove the mask and hope that the general air stream had sufficient oxygen, which very fortunately proved to be the case.

The Sewerage Board accepted our recommendation, which was to line the sewer with a thin-walled glass fibre reinforced plastic (GRP) pipe and to inject the annular space with cement grout to form a composite structure. As well as the existing east bank trunk sewer, construction was under way on a new trunk sewer for the city's development on the west bank, to convey sewage to a new treatment works on that side of the river. Being of similar concrete construction to the failing east bank sewer, we recommended that the sections which already been constructed should be retrofitted with a new liner before they were put into use.

For the sections that were not yet constructed, we proposed an amendment to the design in which the concrete was cast against a flexible sheet of PVC laid on top of the circular former and mechanically keyed into the concrete once hardened, taking advantage of a new product on the market, Ameron T-lock, designed for just this kind of application.

The trunk sewer lining contract was a first of its kind and needed a contractor who was well organised, with adequate resources and ideas. It was awarded to Baroudi Awad, a local firm but of Palestinian origin. They did an excellent job, their managing director, Nabil Awad, took a close personal interest and meetings were productive and business-like. The liner pipes themselves were made in a factory in Dubai and brought up to Baghdad by road.

Sewerage & Sewage Treatment Master Plan

It was 1980 and Saddam was in full 'spend spend spend' mode. With generous funding from central government, the Baghdad Sewerage Board had embarked upon a massive programme of new sewerage and treatment plant construction, but on the basis of very rudimentary planning. Acknowledging this, they obtained bids from three consulting firms to produce a Master Plan for sewerage and sewage treatment, to align with a general master plan for the city's development that had been prepared in 1973 by Polish state consulting service, Polservice. That plan anticipated the city growing to a population of 4.3 million by the year 2000.

We were successful in being awarded what was a prestigious project for the firm, but it had to be completed to a very tight timescale. With construction already under way in accordance with the Board's own hurriedly prepared preliminary designs, they were anxious to arrive at a more carefully considered and longer term plan as soon as possible. We assembled a team of five or six engineers and technicians to undertake the collection and collation of basic data on the existing assets, operational conditions, flow records, biological and chemical analyses etc.

The data capture phase was proceeding apace in September 1980 when we were interrupted by forces outside of our control, namely the outbreak of hostilities between Iraq and its neighbour Iran, to the east. This incident and its effect on life in the city is recalled in another chapter, at this point suffice it to say that, after a bit of a pause, work did continue on the Master Plan, and we did manage to complete it, albeit that there were some additional administrative issues that restricted what we could do.

The Plan was a very important document for the BSB and under normal circumstances we would have expected comments and queries to be addressed and rounds of meetings. We didn't 'workshop' a draft as might be more typical with such a key document. However the situation that we found ourselves in was unique and the Board were relieved and grateful that we actually managed to deliver it. Before the team left Baghdad we had some general discussions with the Board's engineers on our initial thinking and ideas, but once back in Leeds we got down to detailed computations and proceeded straight to the final issued report. Production of the report was greatly aided by the appearance in the office of the first word processing typewriter and a new employee, Linda, who got the best out of it. They were a godsend.

In common with other cities in the Middle East, in 1980 Baghdad had a separate system of foul sewers and surface water drains. The Middle East is a dry region – in the Gulf states annual rainfall is about a sixth of that of London, which itself is in the driest corner of the UK. Baghdad is not quite so arid, it experiences about 50% more total rain per annum than in the Gulf and it has twice as many wet days. I didn't think to question the separate sewer convention, which was based on sound hydraulic engineering principles, until I was taken to see a main surface water sewer, well notionally that it is what it was supposed to be, but it was a dry day and it was conveying a considerable flow of oily sanitary waste. The BSB also recognised this for what it was and had devised a controlled cross connection that enabled that liquid to be diverted into the main foul trunk sewer during dry weather.

Full segregation of foul waste and surface waters in a separate system is never 100% in even the best regulated systems, but in Baghdad it was much less than that and if we were developing a Master Plan for dealing with sanitary wastes, it didn't seem to me to be reasonable simply to assume that all of the incorrect connections of foul sewage into the surface water sewers would be tracked down and eliminated. How would that be done? How much would it cost? Although we were not required to address surface water drainage, it came to us and we couldn't ignore it.

In the last 20 years or so, UK design practice in surface water drainage has changed markedly. It is common practice now to incorporate attenuation mechanisms so as to minimise conduit sizes and avoid increasing the risk of flooding further downstream in the catchment. But in 1980, standard design methods in the UK had not advanced much from those of the 1930s, attenuation was the exception rather than the rule.

Realising that the flat landscape of Baghdad provided a possible opportunity to incorporate detention storage throughout a combined system, we set about investigating if and how it could be made to work. One of our competitors, Ward Ashcroft and Parkman, had acquired the UK licence for surface water drainage design from German consultants Dorsch Consult. Crucially, Dorsch's Hydrograph Volume Method (HVM) was able properly to model a surcharged sewerage system which the standard UK design methods of the day could not. Our collaboration with Ward Ashcroft (through its subsidiary company GECS) and Dorsch bore fruit. We developed a single pipe combined sewer design that incorporated moderately over-sized sewers, with larger and more numerous manholes, and which accepted that there would be shallow surface water flooding in flat streets during heavy rainfall. All future designs that we produced were based on this model.

A problem with a combined system in such climates is the evaporation of water seals in surface water gullies, giving rise to odour nuisance. Taking advantage of the abundance of water that was then available in the mighty River Tigris flowing through the city, we designed a road gully that had an extra deep water seal. River water was already used for irrigating the city's landscaped areas, delivered both by a pipe network and bowser trucks, so that operation could readily be extended to top up gully traps. If a city resident was affected by odour from a particular gully, it could be solved simply with a bucket or two of water.

In the never ending battle of ordinary man *vs* the bureaucracy, a small victory for the former may be recorded at this point. Our gully design incorporated a special plastic fabrication and a contract for bulk supply of these items was awarded to a UK company, Hepworth Plastics. When Hepworth's director came to sign the contract, BSB asked to see his Power of Attorney, which he had not thought to bring. With presence of mind, the Hepworth sales representative, who was well known to us and to the BSB, came into our office and wrote one out for his boss. It was accepted.

Design and Construction Supervision

Once the Master Plan report was accepted, we had the task of designing elements that weren't covered by the contracts that had already been let by the BSB. There were many kilometres of sewer and the number of construction plans and longitudinal sections that would be required was somewhat daunting. A simple back of the envelope calculation showed that our drawing office capacity would be overwhelmed, which led us for the first time to contemplate and then embrace the brave new world of computer-aided design and drafting (CAD).

At that time we did not possess a computer in the office, let alone a plotter to produce drawings or software to drive it. The launch of the IBM PC which altered that dynamic for good was still to come. There were specialists out there, however, and we entered into an agreement with one of them, SIA. Although their software at the time didn't perform any hydraulic designs, it did undertake all of the geometric computations and logic checking prior to plotting out the longitudinal profile sections needed for construction. The quality of the drawings that were produced, at a rate of 50 or more per week at the peak, was excellent.

It was to their credit that the BSB had managed to launch tenders, appoint contractors and get construction under way on such a scale, a total of 27 contracts representing expenditure in excess of $500m. They were let on a design and construct basis to a wide range of contractors – local Iraqi and Kuwaiti, Indian, Japanese, German, Austrian and French, the latter, Degremont, being in joint venture with Iraq's State Contracting Company for a new sewage treatment works at Kerkh to serve the west bank of the city. They had done so using their in house engineers, supplemented by two engineers who had been seconded to them by Polservice.

The Board realised that it could not possibly manage the supervision of the projects with its existing complement of staff plus two Polish ex-pats. We were successful in being awarded a commission to provide about 40 resident contract advisers, most of whom were site based. My original Section Leader at Haiste, Andrew Fountain, was appointed as Haiste's manager in Iraq. John Haiste, a descendant once or twice removed of the firm's founder, took on the job of working in the BSB office with Yan Skuza and his colleague Marian from Polservice, to review the detailed designs that were submitted by the Baghdad contractors. I was in charge of head office back up.

At that time Iraq had good diplomatic relationships with the Soviet Union and its satellite states, many Iraqi state organisations were supported by advisers from these countries. Their citizens were generally happy to work in what many from the west would have regarded as a hardship post, at a lower salary than their western counterparts, as it gave them access to hard currency. A few used the opportunity to defect to the west.

John Haiste recalls his fascination when coming across eastern bloc engineering practices for the first time. Generally their technology was based on a 'massive is good' approach with little concept of economic design. Yan and Marian's bible was a Polish design book which to us was out-dated, but it was a comprehensive tome for which we had no UK equivalent within a single reference and it served as a helpful starting point for discussion. Our Polish counterparts were reluctant to depart from their script, after all they had to answer to their superiors and if they adhered to it they could not be criticised. It was a struggle sometimes to persuade them to adopt anything different when there was a solution that we perceived as more appropriate to local conditions.

Contractors were free to use recognised norms such as British Standards, German DIN, American ASTM or other acceptable international standards. However it wasn't long before it became apparent that the application of different standards could sometimes result in significantly different outcomes for the same element, none more so than in the design of large diameter concrete pipelines. Each contractor was following established practice in the designer's country of origin and we could not reject a design which would not have been passed in the UK, if it was in line with practice in another country whose standards were deemed to be contractually valid. One of Haiste's most experienced structural engineers, Gunnar Kronbachs, originally from Latvia, helped me considerably in getting to grips with the differences in design approach. I came to the conclusion that, the UK design approach gave the highest factor of safety, followed in descending order by that of the USA, then Japan, and the least Germany.[13]

We had the greatest difficulty in approving the designs of German contractor, Ed Züblin of Stuttgart, and whilst there was no contractual basis for seeking any amendment, we did feel some justification for the reservations that we expressed when a length of 3m diameter precast concrete sewer cracked during backfilling of the trench. The pipes themselves were manufactured to a high standard in a purpose built factory in Baghdad, equipped with the same machinery that was used to make pipes in Germany. The design code was satisfactory when construction was executed in Germany under a tight quality control regime, but notwithstanding the senior German personnel that the contractor fielded in Baghdad, the quality of the workforce and supervisory control on the site was not of the same level and shortcomings in that aspect was the reason for the structural failure.

Another technical issue that was the source of considerable controversy concerned the rigidity, or "specific stiffness" of glass reinforced plastic (GRP) sewer pipes, that corrosion resistant material being ideally suited to foul sewers in the intermediate size range, 400 to 1000 mm diameter. In the low stiffness camp (typically 1,000 – 2,000 N/mm^2), were the several companies whose pipes were made by filament winding and comprised only glass and resin. In the high stiffness camp (typically 10-12,000 N/mm^2), was the sole producer of thicker walled pipes made by centrifugal spinning of chopped glass fibre together with fine sand and resin. Filament wound pipes were cheaper than centrifugally spun in the low stiffness range, whereas the opposite was the case at higher stiffness. It wasn't surprising to find manufacturers aligning themselves with the theories that were commercially advantageous for them.

Pressure from the company representatives was quite intense, not just on us, but on the clients too. I knew that whatever we recommended would result in a backlash of some nature from the disappointed pipe manufacturer(s), especially as opting for a high stiffness pipe favoured one particular manufacturer, whereas low stiffness pipes were available from several.

After much personal research and discussions with the competing firms, I felt that I was getting to grips with the subject[14] and I was in the throes of preparing a carefully considered report that would make a recommendation, when the BSB took matters into their own hands. In characteristic market place haggling mode leading to a deal, they decided to specify GRP pipes of 5,000 N/mm^2 stiffness. It satisfied neither camp, but it was a decision and we could get on with it, and it removed any whiff of corruption that might have emerged if one or the other camp had been favoured.

Operation and maintenance

After initial commissioning and passing the formal tests on completion, it was typical practice in the procurement of a treatment plant for there to be a period of trial operation by the contractor, during which various control adjustments would be made to optimise the process and to demonstrate that the plant was capable of meeting the specified performance criteria. Client personnel received training in the plant's operation, but it assumed that the workforce had the necessary basic skills to be able to benefit fully from the contractor's instructions. This led to our being awarded a commission from the BSB to provide complementary skills training and general back up support in operational matters. Our man for this task was Edwin Arthur ('Teddie') Drew, OBE, a civil engineer and a Past President of the Institute of Public Health Engineers.

In the year that I was born, Teddie had been serving as a naval officer during WWII when his ship, HMS Cornwall, was attacked by a Japanese dive bomber. The vessel sank after only 22 minutes with the loss of 198 men. Covered in heavy fuel oil, Teddie managed to stay alive in shark infested waters for 26 hours until he was picked up by HMS Enterprise. He went on to serve in the Arctic Convoys[15].

After the war, Teddie had risen through the civilian ranks to become Chief Engineer for the Middle Lee Regional Drainage Scheme, where he oversaw the construction and operation of the large Rye Meads sewage treatment works to the north of London. He had good reason to boast of the quality of effluent from his works – fish could be found swimming in the final settlement tank effluent launders. In staffing up for the works operation, Teddie recruited former naval personnel who had looked after ships' engines and pumps and were ideally suited to the role of skilled operatives on a large sewage treatment plant.

After retiring from the Drainage Board, Teddie became a consultant and senior adviser to our firm. For the Baghdad commission he brought together a small team of his former workforce and others of a similar background to train BSB personnel. Many of them were ex-military, including some sub-mariners, however they were accustomed to well organised and disciplined support facilities and chains of command which we and the BSB could not match. It led to a certain amount of frustration with their employment conditions and their "advisory only" functions.

It became a casualty of the war of attrition that the conflict with Iran developed into, as more and more Iraqi men were called up for military service and BSB personnel who had been trained were conscripted. The commission had to be drawn to a premature close when, in effect, our trainers were spending more and more of their time undertaking the tasks that BSB personnel should have been doing.

Jaunts for the boys

One of the perks that Iraqi clients' senior staff hoped for when there were foreign companies employed by their organisation, was to get a place on a fact-finding trip out of the country, preferably to Europe. We arranged several such trips, usually but not always including visits to our office and presentations of various kinds there, and to the premises of suppliers of relevant products and equipment.

One trip that remains firmly in my memory was organised for the Deputy Director of the BSB, Anwar Altrachki, together with senior civil engineer Papken Markarian, an Iraqi of Armenian origin, and Mohammed, their senior mechanical engineer based at the Rustamiyah sewage treatment works. After one of my regular visits to Iraq, I left Baghdad in the company of our three clients to accompany them on the trip. The first stop was at Hamburg, where we were to visit a factory making PVC lined concrete pipes, a relatively new product at that time, one which we had recommended to the Board in our report on sewer corrosion.

We arrived at the hotel and were advised that, unfortunately, there had been some slip up in the booking – they only had two rooms for us, doubles but with single beds. Immediately Papken declared that he and Mohammed would share one room. Anwar didn't object to sharing with me, it was just for the one night and we were tired.

In contrast to the somewhat dour Papken, Mohammed was always smiling and joking. Next morning, he was especially cheerful and confided in me that, after a quick turn around in their room, he and Papken had headed off to the Reeperbahn to enjoy some of the night services on offer there. It was obvious that the two of them had been planning it en-route and that their boss wouldn't have been included, so neither wanted to share a room with him. After an interesting few hours at the pipe factory and the hospitality provided there, we left Hamburg and reverted to normal sleeping arrangements on the next stop over.

Amer was a young Iraqi engineer, not long out of university but put in charge of a large sewerage contract, a heavy level of responsibility for someone with such limited experience, even with one of our advisers to support him. He was fortunate and deserving of being picked for a place on a visit to Europe. At one point he was staying in Leeds over the weekend and unaccompanied, so when I asked him if he would like to see some of the country he expressed a particular wish to go to the seaside, as he had never before seen the sea.

We set off for Scarborough and enjoyed a pleasant drive until a couple of miles from the coast when we encountered a thick bank of fog, the infamous east coast 'haar'. I parked the car on the cliff top above the south beach, but although we could hear the waves and smell the salty air, the sea wasn't visible until we descended to shore level where he got his first sighting and smiled broadly. After a walk along the front and having worked up a bit of an appetite, a stop for traditional fish and chips was a no-brainer and was well received.

Official recognition

Several years of work overseas, much of it in Iraq and Libya, employing more than a hundred engineers and technicians and earning foreign exchange that made a small contribution towards balancing the nation's books, was duly recognised in 1982 in the form of a Queen's Award for Export. I reproduce here the key words of the citation, an accolade of which I and my colleagues were justifiably proud. A copy hangs on the wall behind my desk.

ELIZABETH THE SECOND

By the Grace of God of the United Kingdom of Great Britain and Northern Ireland and of our other Realms and Territories Queen Defender of the Faith to

HAISTE INTERNATIONAL LIMITED

Greeting!

We being cognisant of the outstanding achievement of the said body and manifested in the furtherance and increase of the Export Trade of our United Kingdom of Great Britain and Northern Ireland. Our Channel Islands and our Island of Man and being desirous of showing our Royal Favour do hereby confer upon it

THE QUEEN'S AWARD FOR EXPORT ACHIEVEMENT

By the Sovereign's Command

Margaret Thatcher (signature)

The Queen's Representative, the Lord Lieutenant of the County of Yorkshire, presented the award to the company's directors. The press turned up to take part in the celebrations and Richard Whiteley, latterly of Countdown fame but then a front man on Yorkshire Television, recorded an interview for Calendar, YTV's teatime news programme.

7 Expatriate Life in Iraq

When he was casting around for an overseas posting in the late 1970s, John Falkingham recalls that he had two offers – in Saudi Arabia with our competitors, Watsons, and with us in Najaf-Kufa in Iraq. A bit of research in his local library (pre-internet days of course) soon revealed to him that although they were both Muslim countries, life in Iraq might require a bit less of a cultural adjustment than a move to Saudi Arabia, where the rulers were of the Wahhabi sect and exercised tight control.

In Iraq, Christians were free to worship and could hold positions of seniority in state and municipal organisations. Foreign Minister Tariq Azziz, who became a familiar face during the diplomatic encounters that preceded the 2003 Iraq war, was Christian. Although still very much a patriarchal society, women could be found in executive roles and were able to drive. The wearing of headscarf (hijab) or full cloak (abaya) was a matter for personal or family choice. The availability of alcoholic beverages was another difference.

Getting in and out

At that time a standard Iraqi entry visa was valid for only two weeks. If one had to remain beyond two weeks it was necessary to register at the Residents' Office and have the passport stamped accordingly. A letter of support from the organisation with which one was engaged in the country was required. Beyond four weeks you were deemed to be resident and a whole new set of regulations kicked in, the most significant of which was the requirement for an exit visa to be able to leave the country, this time requiring a letter of release from the sponsoring organisation. It led to many anxious moments for expatriates, who were beholden to their Iraqi counterparts when wishing to take leave of absence or depart permanently at the end of an employment contract.

A visit to the Residents' Office involved proceeding from one office to another and from window to window to conclude the several stages required to get the essential stamp. One's passport would be taken away at certain points and given the sheer numbers of passports being processed, there was some nail biting until that beautiful little blue booklet was safely back in your hands.

As the numbers of foreigners in the country increased, the Residents' Office struggled to cope. It was not just engineers and other professionals, the Iraqi labour force was out-numbered by workers brought in by international contractors from the Indian sub-continent and the far east. Contractors' agents could be seen arriving with large bundles of passports to be processed, but at some point during the war with Iran the authorities decided in their wisdom that everyone had to attend in person. Chaos ensued as crowds of foreigners massed around the Office and filled the corridors and rooms. I recall being in a crush and finding myself squeezed up against the only woman in a noisy and packed corridor of men, a lady from Greece who was becoming increasingly distressed. We got her outside and managed to find a Greek man who was able to assist, eventually we got the passports stamped.

There were three different offices, one that dealt with western countries, another for the Arab states, and a third for the Indian sub-continent and the far east. It was bad enough for us when the new rule came in, but there was a massive increase at the far east office when waves of Indian and Philippino site labourers turned up. If we thought that we had had a hard day at the office, it was much worse for our counterparts from the Japanese contractors who worked on our schemes.

Haiste partner Bernard Eagles gamed the system a few times by arranging to have ten days or so in Iraq, then leaving for Kuwait, say, for a few days, to attend to business there, then returning to Iraq for another spell before heading back home to the UK.

An option for a sojourn out of Iraq was to stop off in Beirut, where our Iraqi representative had relatives and there were genuine marketing leads that could be followed up. A cosmopolitan city on the Mediterranean coast, a few days spent in Lebanon's capital was generally rather enjoyable. The climate was more benign than in central and southern Iraq, and to take a day trip out of Beirut into the Bekaa valley, where the air was clear and fresh, vineyards could be visited and delicious fresh fruit obtained, was a pleasure. The down side of the trip was George Azzouz's driving, he flung his Mercedes with abandon around the snaking mountain roads. With sheer drops and paucity of Armco barriers, I just shut my eyes and prayed.

Civil war broke out in Lebanon in 1977. On a previous occasion we had stayed in an apartment, but during the civil war luxury hotels like the Carlton were virtually empty. When Bernard Eagles and I stayed there the ratio of hotel residents to staff was probably about one to one – no problem to catch the eye of the waiter at dinner. The Carlton was opposite George Azzouz's apartment and both exhibited damage from mortar fire, his balcony having taken a direct hit. During fighting, George and his family moved down to the basement and lived there until the warring militias moved on to another area of the city in the battle for territorial control.

Cars, houses and domestic arrangements

As a visitor to Iraq, an international driving licence was needed to be permitted to drive, readily obtainable in the UK from the AA or RAC on production of one's UK driving licence. For expatriates living in Iraq, however, a local licence was necessary and this required the Iraqi driving test to be passed. The main part of the test involved manoeuvring around a test track marked out by cones, if none of the cones were touched then it was a pass.

The layout of the cones was the same regardless of the size of car and for our Najaf Assistant Adviser, John Falkingham, well over six feet in height and having chosen a fairly large car, a Toyota Cressida, it was deemed to be a bit of a challenge when it came to the cones test. He squeezed himself into a borrowed Toyota Corolla and got through.

When we obtained the commission for the supervision of sewerage works in Baghdad, a huge logistical and administrative operation got under way. We had to acquire transport for an additional 40 engineers, and housing for them and their families, as the majority came out on a married basis. We were indebted to long time Haiste employee, Alan Macdonald, who took on the role of assistant manager to Andrew Fountain and was in charge of all administrative matters.

Alan had prior overseas working experience and was a steadying influence in dealing with the various bureaucratic arms of the Iraq state. Never flustered or giving up on an apparently intractable problem, he presented a reassuring face to the many newcomers that the firm recruited and who were first-timers in that situation. One of his rules was to treat all local counterparts as 'friends', regardless of their attitude towards him and our circumstances, never to get on the wrong side of them or display annoyance or anger however justified it may be. There were enough problems to be overcome without making enemies that could easily make some aspect of life impossible.

When we needed to bring in more than 40 new cars our first approach was to British Leyland, which had a strong presence in Baghdad through the supply and maintenance of the double-decker buses that offered transport to the masses in the city, one of the legacies of decades of British influence. We would have liked to have to bought British, just as employees of German, Italian and French companies would be seen around in Opels, Fiats and Peugeots. However for that ailing company it all seemed too difficult to deliver what we wanted at a reasonable price and timescale, so we fell back on the default choice of a batch of Toyota Coronas, which had basic air conditioning and a reputation for reliability that wasn't matched by the Morris Marina. Included in the deal with Toyota was a Crown model for Andrew Fountain. The Toyotas turned out to be robust and withstood considerable abuse.

Foreign companies were able to import cars duty free and were separately registered with a different colour and style of registration plate to locally owned vehicles. Having managed to get them through customs, our cars were held in a compound until registration formalities were concluded and the number plates had been made and delivered. There was some frustration with the cars having been paid for but not yet released for use on the road, meantime our first few contract advisers were already in post and had to rely upon contractors' vehicles to be picked up from home and taken to site.

Eventually the documentation was concluded and the number plates were delivered for fixing onto the cars, but in a final irritant in the saga, the sets of plates, i.e. in excess of 80 individual items, were tipped from a small truck in a heap. Alan Macdonald's first task was to have to sort them into matching pairs!

Cars were imported for the use of and in the names of individual employees. Unforeseen at the time of original importation was a sting in the tail. When an employee left Iraq at the end of his contract, the options were either to surrender the car to the authorities, or to have it exported and sold in the Kuwait second hand market. It could not simply be transferred to somebody else. Cars had a hard life and after a few years some were in better condition than others. A car that was due to be exported might have been in good condition whereas a continuing staff member might have a wreck. This necessitated much swapping of parts, even engines being transposed which meant filing off numbers on the engine block and re-stamping numbers! An offence if discovered.

With a high demand from international companies, finding acceptable accommodation for staff was not an easy task. Inevitably there were differences and as anyone who follows Kirsty and Phil in "Location Location Location" knows, compromises have to be made. Some advisers were fussier than others and of course their wives came into it too. In writing this nearly forty years later I am acutely conscious that in describing the male employee as breadwinner, with wife domestically engaged at home is not necessarily how things are now, but it's how it was then. Andrew and Alan had to find ways to balance things out, so that, for example, a house that was not so good in location or accommodation would be better furnished and equipped to compensate.

Although in Iraq the position of women in society was better than in some other states in the region, a line was drawn at co-habitation. Adrian Pyrah was our mechanical engineer adviser and he was with Linda whom he wished to join him in Baghdad. It was simply not possible for her to obtain a visa and be a resident of Iraq, as an unmarried foreign woman who was not an employee within the framework of a contract with a state entity. The solution was to get married, which they did in the splendid surroundings of the British Embassy, at that time situated in prime position on the banks of the River Tigris.

With expatriate staff resident in the country, anyone travelling out there from the UK was likely to have to bring in items that could not be obtained on the local market, bacon being high on the list. Even if there was no specific request, a vacuum pack or two was always a well received gift when accepting the hospitality of an expatriate at his home. Porridge oats and Marmite were other consumables that I recall packing into my suitcase. Video tapes filled with UK TV programmes was another favourite, although their confiscation by customs officials was always a possibility.

Audio cassettes with western music were readily available in the markets, albeit not necessarily the latest issues and more likely than not pirated copies. One that was not obtainable, since it was banned by the Iraqi authorities but which I brought in at Stuart Ashton's request, was Boney M's rendition of "Rivers of Babylon", a huge pop hit throughout Europe in 1978, with "Brown Girl in the Ring" almost equally popular on the B side. The reason for the banning was simple – the opening lines and chorus of the lyrics were:

"By the rivers of Babylon, there we sat down,
Ye-eah we wept, when we remembered Zion"

In Saddam's Iraq, Christians were free to practice their faith openly, which might include attending church, but very few Jews remained. The state of Israel was not recognised and the Iraqi state propaganda machine kept up a steady flow of invective.

Eating and drinking

In Libya, a colleague who worked in that country informed me that it was quite possible to consume a diet that was well balanced, over the period of a year. Frozen chickens, for example, could be absent from the market place for a period of time, then reappear in a glut at which point everyone rushed out to stock up and replenish their freezers. Such 'feast and famine' was nowhere near as pronounced in Iraq as far as the basic staples were concerned, although regularly some unfamiliar imported produce would suddenly appear on the shelves of every corner shop. Tinned processed cheese and Bulgar beans come to mind in that regard.

In Baghdad there were three or four breweries, producing beers of the Pilsner type. In order of general preference the Brits tended to favour the Shaharazad brand, followed by Ferida which was more commonly available. If these were out of stock the Golden brand was tolerable, but Lulu was drunk only if there was nothing else on offer. To purchase a supply of beer for domestic consumption cash alone was insufficient, filled bottles were exchanged for empties. One of the priorities of a new arrival therefore was to source and buy a crate of empty bottles from someone leaving or with an excess.

At one time Iraq was the world's leading producer of dates, so not surprising perhaps that their distilleries produced arak spirit made from that fruit. Like ouzo and other similar anise flavoured drinks, it goes cloudy with the addition of water or ice. The Iraqi arak came in plain, clear glass screw topped bottles with imprinted lettering that would not have looked out of place on a kitchen shelf of cleaning fluids. It was a bit on the firewatery side for my liking.

After some initial stays at the Baghdad Hotel, we transferred our allegiance to the Abu Nawas Hotel, which was situated on the street of that name, on the edge of the central business district and with a view of the River Tigris. Named after a famous 8th century Arab poet, it was a more modern hotel than the Baghdad and it suited us better in many respects, although the dinner menu became a bit repetitive. Even more repetitive was the sole cassette tape that was played to diners, in a loop, comprising a collection of early rock and roll tracks from the 1950s, Jerry Lee Lewis et al. Some of those I still find moderately catchy, but Bill Haley's *"Rock Around the Clock"* is not one and it became somewhat of an irritant. If it is played on the radio, which thankfully is rare these days, I am immediately taken back to that time and place.

In the early days decent restaurants were few in number, until the increased crude oil income started to have an impact on the numbers of foreigners in the city and hotels like the Sheraton and Meridian opened with their fine dining rooms. It was on one of my early trips to Baghdad that I first experienced a chilled beer being served in a frosted dimple glass that had been kept in the freezer. There were times when one had difficulty arguing that an assignment in Baghdad constituted a hardship posting!

My personal favourite dining treat was to have what is often regarded as the Iraqi national dish, masgûf, river fish of the carp family caught in the Tigris and then barbecued on vertical skewers against a driftwood fire. There were several establishments along the river bank that prepared the dish, which was always fresh since the fish were kept alive in large glass sided tanks from which one could make a selection, of a size appropriate to the number in your party. The fish was removed and killed and a numbered brass tag was attached to identify it as yours.

Whilst one could eat at the riverside establishment, it was common to have it taken to another restaurant nearby, such as the Abu Nawas, that may offer better comfort and where starters and desserts could be taken to complete the meal. The fish was presented opened out on a large platter on top of flat bread with a few garnishes and eaten with the fingers. A considerate host might invite you to take a piece of the delicate white flesh from just behind the head, considered to be the best tasting part.

Off duty

British expatriates who lived in the empire and colonies often established a club where they could socialise in a manner redolent of life back home, membership being generally closed to the indigenous population. Clubs typically offered recreational and sporting facilities as well as a kitchen able to produce traditional dishes out of the home cook book, subject to the availability of suitable local or imported produce.

A very fine club of this nature was thriving in the Alwiyah district of Baghdad, when the 1958 revolution overturned the established order and British administrators and governmental advisers had to leave the country. It was reconstituted however, for the benefit of Iraqis of the new elite, and was renamed The Alwiyah Club. I was hosted there once as a guest of our local representative and was impressed by the well tended facilities and the formal 'silver service' dining experience, which seemed to be carrying on the tradition of the previous regime.

At some point further down the line, when Brits were no longer *personae non grata*, they were permitted to set up another club, rather less grand and certainly less formal than its colonial era predecessor. This became The New British Club and was the centre of the social scene for British expats in the city. As well as a bar and catering, it had an excellent swimming pool and a large garden.

As you would expect of an establishment of this nature, there was a framed picture of our monarch on prominent display. However it was also obligatory for all premises to have a picture of Iraq's president, latterly Saddam Hussein, and when its absence was noted on one occasion by a functionary of the state, the club manager was persuaded to rectify the omission and toe the line. He did so, hanging the picture of Hussein on the same wall as but below that of Queen Elizabeth II.

On my first visits to Iraq, portraits could be seen both of the incumbent president, Ahmed Hassan al-Bakr, and his powerful deputy, Saddam Hussein, but after 1979 when the latter ousted the former, al-Bakr's images were soon taken down. For many years afterwards, however, on the side of a commercial building on Sadoun Street, the outline of Abu Bakr's head in profile could still be discerned, picked out in a fading neon light, somehow having been overlooked in the political cleansing regime.

British citizens living in Baghdad could join the club as full members; those living in one of the provincial towns or cities outside of Baghdad could be country members and paid a reduced subscription to reflect their less frequent attendance, which generally would be limited to weekends (Fridays). Visiting non resident Brits like me could also join, as extraordinary country members.

Renewal of membership was a formality provided that there had been no report of anti-social behaviour or other infringement of the club rules. Fees became due annually, but if an extraordinary country member wasn't in the country at the due date it was simply a matter of payment on the first available occasion. I turned up at the club on such a visit, ready to pay my sub, only to be told that the committee had withdrawn my membership and I could not enter. The decision had been reached in closed session on the basis of a report by a member, who alleged that I had been seen in the club at a time when my subscription payment was overdue. To make things worse I had supposedly defaced the notice on which was listed the names of those members! Due to the level of commercial activity in the country, the committee at the time had imposed a limit on membership numbers. With a wait list there was every motivation to bar a member who had stepped out of line and replace him with a new one, who would contribute a joining fee to the club coffers as well as an annual subscription.

I was informed that the fabricated report had come from one of our employees, who I shall not name. I must have incurred his displeasure in some way, although I never did find out what had irked him, but instead of raising it with me or with Andrew Fountain, our local manager, he chose this way to get his own back. I was annoyed and disappointed that a British club should bar a member without being given the opportunity to deny or explain the incident. I penned a strong letter of protest. It was a stupid allegation as it was clear from the entry and exit stamps in my passport that I was not in Iraq at the time. I received an apology and my membership was restored. I do not recall what action, if any, was taken against my complainant, fortunately the scheme that he was supervising was running smoothly and did not need me to visit it. I made a point of avoiding confrontation, confining myself to any necessary discussions with Andrew.

Weekends could also be passed in pleasant manner by visiting historic sites. For archaeological interest the Arch of Ctesiphon was within easy reach of Baghdad, the spiral minaret at Samarra and the Hanging Gardens of Babylon also being feasible for day trips. Lake Habbaniyah, a drive of an hour or so out of Baghdad, was a popular spot. Boating on the lake was possible and on one occasion a race of self-build crafts was organised amongst the expatriate community, with keen competition amongst the companies with resident staff in country. Messrs Falkingham and Moore launched "Pride of Najaf" at this event, in the form of a raft with flotation realised by means of an assembly of pipes and drums, but it proved to be a bit of a handful both to steer and to propel at reasonable speed and our crew failed to get onto the winners' podium.

8 Conflicts in the Middle East

Iraq-Iran War

It was 22nd September 1980. My wristwatch was playing up and after work I took a trip into Baghdad's main shopping and markets area to purchase an inexpensive but hopefully more reliable replacement. I could have purchased one of the many timepieces that were being offered with an image of a benign Saddam Hussein on the dial face, but instead I opted for a less flashy item. In the souk I became aware that something was afoot as the television news was attracting greater than usual interest, but I returned to my hotel and after a meal there I went to bed.

Early next morning I was woken by the sounds of aircraft and gun fire. The hotel that I was in at the time was relatively new, with large windows overlooking the east (left) bank of the River Tigris just a block or two away. I was on an upper floor and had a grandstand view of 'bomb alley' as planes from the Iranian Air Force swept down low over the river to discharge their ordnance onto the Rashid army camp on the east bank and the Doura oil refinery on the west bank.

I was looking down on the roofs of the houses where occupants had been sleeping. It was quite common practice to sleep on a bed on the roof during summer, being cooler at night than inside the house. Not everyone had air conditioning. A number of men were armed with rifles and shot somewhat pointlessly at the planes as they streaked across.

I realised that I wasn't in the safest of places, especially with the glass walls of my room, so I got dressed quickly and went downstairs into the lobby, where I met colleagues staying at the same hotel. We agreed that it would be prudent to move away from that location and so we drove to the house of Iraq manager, Andrew Fountain, where others had also gathered and we held our own council of war. Hotel accommodation was in short supply in Baghdad at that time so we had little hope of finding another hotel straight away and for a night or two a few of us camped out in the houses of our resident advisors.

Our immediate reaction was to want to get out of the country as soon as possible, but that wasn't feasible. Baghdad international airport was closed and military road blocks started to appear, especially on main highway routes out of the city. From Baghdad, the only viable road route out of the country was across the desert to Amman, Jordan, and for a while that too was out of use.

A trip to Hanna Azzouz's office found it to be open and to my delight the telex machine was operational. A short message was sent to the Leeds office for relaying to the relatives of our staff, to confirm that we were all safe. The message was headed "Shaken but not Stirred".

The intensity of that first morning's bombardment was not sustained. The frequency of air raids dropped away as the Iranians used up the stock of spares that they had for their American made Phantom 'planes, reducing the number of aircraft that were fit for combat. Following the overthrow of the Shah and the hostage crisis at the American embassy in Tehran, which was still in progress at the outbreak of war, no more spares were forthcoming from the aircrafts' country of origin. In contrast, Iraq was equipped with Russian MIGs and had no corresponding supply chain issues.

After a few days, some vehicles left the city for Amman, in convoys, but in limited numbers; getting a place on a bus or car was difficult. Some members of our team were coping with the situation better than others and we pressed hard to get places for those in greatest need. Meantime it kept our mind off things to try get back to doing the jobs that we were all there for, and we settled into a routine.

The air attacks invariably targeted critical installations which we tried to keep clear of. When the air raid siren sounded, if driving around one was obliged to stop the car, get out and find the nearest refuge of some kind, a shop or an office. If on a site constructing one of the trunk sewers, a large concrete pipe offered the ideal shelter until the all clear was given. The fact that it was now possible to leave the city, albeit with difficulty, gave some peace of mind.

A feature of the first few months of the war was the appearance of new American made cars on the city's roads. They were given as a form of compensation to families of young men killed in the conflict. As the war dragged on, with casualties continuing and the wealth of the nation denuding, this practice was brought to an end.

Security generally became much more evident and public offices which we visited to obtain essential information to assist us in our study were often reluctant to release what was valuable to us, even though it was unlikely to be in much demand by the Iranian military. I was thankful that, before the outbreak of hostilities, we had acquired survey plans of the whole of the city and taken them back to our Leeds head office, although even then we knew that if found at the airport baggage check it is likely that they would have been confiscated and the courier subjected to interrogation.

I was the courier for the bulk of the survey plans, rolled up tightly in the bottom of my suitcase and surrounded by dirty clothes. It had been agreed that when we got back to Leeds we would confirm their safe arrival and that their code name was "chocolates". I was driven to the airport by Sami from the Azzouz office, who decided to take a back road route to avoid city centre traffic. Sami wasn't the best of drivers and he chose that day to run into the back of the vehicle in front at a minor road junction that fed onto the main airport road. It was quite a sharp bang with significant damage and it was not going to be resolved quickly.

I needed to catch that plane, and to make things worse a policeman appeared. "Sami, the chocolates!" I said to him. I got out quickly, opened the boot, retrieved my suitcase and proceeded rapidly away from the scene, hoping not to be stopped. I flagged down a car with expat number plates that was heading to the airport and the driver kindly got me away, much to my relief. I arrived at the office the next day with the "chocolates" and telexed Baghdad that the office staff had enjoyed them and expressed their thanks. Many years later, during the first Gulf War, British intelligence officers turned up at our office to seek out the same plans.

After several weeks things had settled to a new normal and while Baghdad airport remained closed, there were regular buses to and from Amman. In a shared taxi the cost was comparable to a short haul flight.

Queues developed at the border crossing and it wasn't open on a 24 hour basis, so it was not uncommon to arrive there on an evening to find it closed and to have to wait and try to get some sleep until it reopened in the early morning. The border crossing is at around 800m above sea level and in the winter months the temperature can drop to near zero. On one of those trips, stuck in a bus without heating, I resorted to the old tramp's trick of using newspapers to supplement the insulation offered by my top coat and other layers of clothing.

Finding good but not over-priced hotel accommodation for visitors like me was difficult at that time. German contractor Ed Züblin was constructing a large diameter trunk sewer on the east bank, they had rented the whole of a small hotel for their resident staff and head office visitors. They had their own cook and other domestic staff and I was pleased when they offered one of the rooms to me. Züblin's staff had a fairly cavalier approach to the Iranian air raids and if the sirens went off during the evening they would go up onto the roof to watch the display. Although we were some distance from the main targets, bits of ordnance could be released off target or a plane could be shot down, so the roof wasn't really the safest place to be.

Züblin staff liked to have their evening meal quite early, then enjoy relaxing with a few beers and quite often play cards until it was time to retire for the night. I had no German at all when I first went there but I picked up a few key phrases including all of the calls in 'Yatzee' which was one of their favourite games and I was able to join in. Behind the bar was a display of spirits which didn't seem ever to be touched, beer being the preferred alcoholic beverage. On one occasion I had had a rather stressful day and a measure of Scotch from one of the bottles would have been rather welcome so I asked if I might have one. You may, but you're not going to like it very much I was told – the bottle's golden contents were not whisky but cold tea, it was decorative only.

The Iranian air attacks were limited and were targeted at strategic installations, there was none of widespread destruction of buildings with which one is depressingly familiar in news footage of current conflicts in the region. Between air raids life went on pretty much as normal and there were very few outward signs of the war when travelling around the city.

One day I decided to chance a visit to the east bank sewage treatment works at Rustamiyah, which was situated in the same general area as the main army camp and military airfield, and on the opposite side of the River Tigris from the Doura oil refinery. The large sludge digestion tanks could easily have looked like fuel storage tanks from the air and the BSB had decided to camouflage them. The painter who was employed had clearly not been on any relevant military course in such matters as his design comprised drab green wavy edged polka dots on a khaki background. If anything the pattern drew the eye towards the tanks rather than them merging into the background.

Trade Mission to Iraq and Jordan

The Iraq-Iran war dragged on, but business life continued as we were still being paid for services provided. There was a general view that there was sufficient oil in the ground to underpin Iraq's economy for the foreseeable future. The UK government felt sufficiently bullish about the situation to support an official trade mission to Iraq, combined with neighbouring Jordan, and covering the water sector.

Naturally we wanted to have a delegate on that mission and I was nominated and accepted. The mission leader was the descendant of a well known and respected early 20th century engineer, who had established an eponymous consulting engineering partnership which had been passed down the family line. Despite having no current business in either country, as far as I was aware, the mission leader had emerged from a selection process of some kind, plucked from the consulting 'establishment' in the London area.

I attended a briefing meeting in London to participate in the planning of the mission and it was readily apparent to those attending which firms were already active in the countries and which were not. The latter would be hoping to provide us with more competition in the consulting sector. Missioners were also drawn from the ranks of materials and equipment suppliers and process plant contractors.

A week or so before we were due to set off there was a flare up, when quite a number of Iranian missiles landed on Baghdad a new development in the conflict. John Haiste recalls: "Explosions in the night were a bit disconcerting. I went to a meeting of British managers at the Embassy when the Ambassador gave a half hour discourse. His advice can be summarised as 'if you have no reason to stay you should go, but if you have no reason to go you should stay' which left most of those present rather confused."

The Foreign Office was consulted and its considered view was that the mission could still proceed. Citing family reasons, the mission leader gave notice that he was no longer able to participate.

Sir William Halcrow and Partners, as Halcrows were known then, had work in Jordan. I received a telephone call from their business development manager and fellow delegate, Brian Boston. "You (Haiste) have more work there than anyone else on the mission, so I suggest that you should be the replacement mission leader. If you agree I will nominate you." I did and he did.

Thus in Iraq I was wheeled into meetings with organisations with whom we already had, if not actual commissions, contacts and relationships of some kind, having the dubious pleasure of introducing them to our competitors. But that down side was countered to some extent by my position as mission leader, which I hoped would bolster our credentials with the clients.

The delegates and support personnel were crowded into one ministry official's office, a large enough room for most meetings, but all of his sofas and chairs were taken and so one delegate sat on a small side table made from a piece of dark brown smoked glass supported on a brass legged frame. As our host was speaking and we listened respectfully in silence, the quiet was shattered, literally, by the sound of breaking glass and the unfortunate sitter landing on his bottom in undignified manner, expletives uttered. An inspection of his posterior revealed no torn clothing or blood, so the debris was duly cleared up and the delegate remained standing for the rest of the session.

We went on to Jordan where we had been before on work finding missions, en-route to and from Iraq, but until then without success. From our dominant position in Iraq the tables were turned with Halcrow, who had ongoing work there. By this time in the UK, Haiste were well on the way to becoming a leading player in water industry telemetry, SCADA and

ICA, and as a result of the mission we secured a prestigious commission from the Water Authority of Jordan to advise them on a new national telemetry system.

We entered into a partnership with Halcrow, who already had familiarity with the relevant physical infrastructure. Although it was apparent to Brian Boston that this was a logical and mutually beneficial collaboration, his boss, Halcrow's partner, seemed less keen when we met back in the UK to discuss how we would frame up the contract between us. He gave the impression that he viewed us as the junior partners and not in the same league as the mighty Halcrow. He was obliged to deal with us, but would rather not have had to, and ideally wanted to keep our slice of the commission cake to as small as possible.

I stepped away from the job at that point and handed it over to my colleagues in Haiste Automation, for whom I had considerable respect and confidence that they would deliver on it.

Gaza

Since the formation of the state of Israel in 1948 and the fleeing of Palestinians to refugee camps, if fighting isn't actually taking place on the small patch of densely populated land that is Gaza, then either it is under threat, to some degree of likelihood, or it is in recovery mode after the last bout of fighting.

The basic facilities of water supply and sanitation have to be provided to the extent that is feasible and through its Relief Works Agency (UNRWA), the United Nations endeavour to support those services, together with its many other roles. In 1993, at around the time of the Oslo peace accord, we obtained a commission from UNRWA to evaluate sanitation conditions and make recommendations for improving and upgrading the existing wastewater treatment plant in Rafah, the southernmost town on the border with Egypt.

I was accompanied by a colleague, Azzedine (Dean) Guesmia. Originally from Algeria, Dean became a British resident and passport holder through marriage. It was essential that we secured the cooperation of the mayor and municipal officers of Rafah, but knowing Dean and the ease with which he formed relationships, I was hopeful that he could smooth the path, which he did, earning the plaudits of UNRWA's local director. I had the satisfaction of knowing that our report was soundly based on good quality data and insight into the workings of the municipality and how services were provided both in the authorised developments and the refugee camps. These camps were not tented villages as might be assumed, but comprised buildings of concrete block construction, with water and electricity connections, not very much different to those lived in by the indigenous population.

The Israeli Defence Force (IDF) had several fenced and walled military bases with watch towers, from which they conducted daily patrols in armoured cars and trucks, making forays into the Palestinian developments to try to seek out and apprehend suspected insurgents. Even within that small and densely populated patch of land, there were several Israeli residential settlements, comprising groups of dwellings within walled enclaves. The IDF provided a high level of security to the settlers, who came in and out of the territory in convoys with armed military protection.

In the event of a serious flare up we had been instructed to proceed quickly to Beach Camp, a UN compound on the Mediterranean shore where we would have been evacuated by sea. Fortunately that didn't prove necessary during the relatively short time that I was there, but one could sense a real tension when passing through the military checks at the heavily fortified border crossing into Israel.

Gulf War

I had left Iraq for new pastures when, in 1991, Saddam Hussein mobilised his forces and invaded Kuwait, so I have no personal experience to recount of the events during that conflict that entailed British nationals being taken as hostages, one of them I learned later having been a friend of mine from university days.

As the Gulf War dragged on, the sanctions imposed on the Iraqi regime had wide effects on day to day living, but in an attempt to alleviate conditions for the population at large, the UN established what was known as the Oil for Food programme. Iraq was permitted to export some of its oil, but in exchange for food imports and not dollars that might otherwise be spent on armaments and/or enrichment of the ruling party's leaders. The programme had a broader scope than just provisions. It included pharmaceutical goods as well as essential spare parts and replacements for critical infrastructure pertinent to public health, such as chlorination equipment at water treatment plants and sewage pumps and parts thereof.

In late 1998 I returned to Baghdad under contract to the UN, to report upon sanitation conditions in the city generally, to evaluate the appropriateness and effectiveness of a recently completed series of repair works that had been funded by the Oil for Food programme at main sewage pumping stations, and to make recommendations for further actions.

I was saddened to see the conditions that were being endured by the city's long suffering residents, with raw sewage in the streets in places, just as it was when I first visited more than twenty years earlier. Rustamiyah Sewage Treatment Works, which served the east bank of the city, was in very poor condition, causing pollution of the Diyala River which received the inadequately treated effluent. The sludge that was taken away by farmers for fertilising and soil conditioning was not adequately stabilised or sterilised, thus providing another route for pathogens to enter the food chain. By contrast however, Kerkh works on the west bank was producing a good effluent, albeit at below its design capacity, and after a sufficient period of 'cold digestion' followed by drying on open beds, the sludge was safe to spread on land which grew crops that were not eaten raw.

Unfortunately Baghdad Sewerage Board's responsibility had been reduced to the treatment works and terminal pumping stations only, leaving all of the other pumping stations and sewers to be operated and maintained by nine separate district municipalities. The problems caused by mechanical and electrical breakdowns were exacerbated by lack of coordinated oversight and understanding of how the system was supposed to operate.

Due to the sanctions, hotels were unable to provide the level of service to visitors that had been available before the conflict. I was put up in what had once been a prestige hotel, the Al Rashid, but where a sombre ambience now prevailed – mains electricity was rationed and there was a bare minimum of lighting; food in the restaurant was limited to a very basic menu. At the threshold of the main lobby the floor tiling had been modified to display an unflattering mosaic image of the then US President, with the caption "Bush is Criminal". It was positioned such that it was almost impossible not to step on it – showing the soles of one's shoes, or throwing a shoe at another person, is considered to be a strong insult in Arab etiquette.

I had two weeks to make my appraisal and present a report and was on track to complete it, but three days before I was due to leave I was informed that Iraq was bracing itself for air attacks by the coalition forces. It followed the Iraqi government ending its cooperation with the UN's Commission that was overseeing the destruction of its weapons of mass destruction. I was advised to leave as soon as I could and so I packed up and headed back home along the desert road to Amman. The intelligence was correct, as operation "Desert Fox" that had the aim of destroying the facilities where it was believed that nuclear, biological and chemical weapons were developed and produced, commenced a few days later.

Before leaving I had to settle my account with the hotel. The bill was split between US dollars and Iraqi dinars. I had to change US dollar travellers' cheques at the nearest bank and the bundles of dinars that I received occupied a large space within my briefcase. When I was first in Iraq in the late 1970s, one dinar backed by oil exports was worth about three US dollars, albeit the currency was not freely tradable. But by the mid 1990s one US dollar would buy around 3,000 dinars.

On one of my first visits to Iraq I was given a one fil coin, one thousandth of a dinar, minted in the year 1959 (Gregorian calendar) and 1379 (Muslim calendar). It was no longer in circulation since the smallest denomination in use by then was 10 fils. It will bring you luck I was told and I kept it with my small change whenever in the country, occasionally producing it for amusement if the conversation turned to money. I still have it, the last time I checked there was just one for sale on eBay, for $88!

9 Athens and Greece

In 1983 my workload continued to be dominated by the high level of activity in Iraq, supplemented from time to time by visits to neighbouring Arab countries, which, in March of that year included presenting a paper on Baghdad sewerage and sewage treatment at a conference in Dubai. I was joint author with my boss Bernard Eagles, and Andrew Fountain joined us in giving our presentation, its slot being immediately after a long mid-day break.

The organisers had arranged a short outing for delegates who wished to visit a nearby facility of some technical interest and it had over-run, so when the afternoon session was due to start and a number of delegates were absent, the Chairman decided to postpone until they had returned, about 15 or 20 minutes later. Bernard opened up for us and the Chairman, who had a set of traffic lights at his command, activated the green light. Andrew then took the rostrum and concluded his piece, but by the time I got to the lectern, the Chairman had already illuminated the amber light. We had rehearsed our presentation especially with regard to timing and I knew that we were keeping to our schedule, but his way of getting the conference schedule back on track was to cut our slot. I could see where it was heading, so I was obliged to skip chunks of my carefully prepared delivery. It didn't seem long after I started when the red light came on, I pressed on to the end, wondering if at any moment a couple of the Chairman's minders would appear and drag me away! Much hard work had gone into our presentation and I felt cheated.

Back in Baghdad afterwards and scheduled to return home, I had a message from Hugh Brooksbank asking me to stop off in Athens en-route, as we had been successful in our bid for the implementation of the Greater Athens Sewage Transportation and Treatment Project. Oh and by the way I had been named in the bid as our Project Manager. I didn't recall having been asked, but there were worse places to have to work. We had secured the commission on the basis of our experience in Baghdad and that of our American joint venture (JV) partners, Woodward Clyde Consultants, who had been responsible for the San Francisco Ocean Outfall Project. They were unknown to me at the time but I was impressed.

The third member of our consortium was local firm Gofas and Partners. A small and wiry man of cheerful disposition, Mr Gofas had a small consultancy specialising in dams and irrigation projects. Leonidas Papanikolou was his junior partner and his only other permanent staff were the two Marias, tracing Maria and typing Maria.

Apostolos Barbastathis was one of the many self-employed Greek engineers who worked on a contract basis, he had been named in the bid documents as one of our team. He met me at the airport and drove me into the city in his Mini Cooper. He took me to the top of Lycabettus Hill, from which vantage point I was able to view the whole of the city's dense sprawl and the location of the proposed wastewater treatment plant just visible in the far distance.

Our client was EYDE, a special department within the Ministry of Public Works set up specifically to execute the project. The office was situated on Odos Varvaki, just off Leoforos Alexandros, a heavily trafficked route that forms part of the city's vehicle restriction cordon, intended to combat pollution in the city centre. Outwardly it gave the appearance of being just another of the low rise residential apartment units in a typical narrow Athens street.

A politicised project

The background to our appointment was a political battle. In the 1970s, the World Bank had financed a master plan and feasibility study for Greater Athens that was undertaken by British consultants, J D & D M Watson (later to become Watson Hawksley, then Montgomery Watson, and now absorbed within Stantec). Their extremely thorough study with its preliminary designs was impressive, comprising several individual reports and plans contained within two large blue boxes. For many years, apart from some largely ineffective screening and grit removal, sewage from the majority of the three million inhabitants of Athens had been discharged untreated into the Saronic Gulf at Akrokeramos, in the district of Keratsini and a short distance to the west of the main port of Piraeus. Parts of the northern suburbs of the city were connected into a sewage works at Metamorphosis that was in operation and due for extension.

Watsons had recommended constructing a treatment works adjacent to the location of the existing outfall, on a site that was hemmed in by a mix of residential, commercial and industrial developments. The proposal was for the waste to receive primary or partial treatment only and for the effluent to be discharged out to sea through a long outfall pipe. Dilution would take place over a wide area and eliminate gross pollution close to the shore line. This approach to the disposal of waste from coastal communities was commonplace around the world at that time. The EEC's Urban Wastewater Directive, which would have required secondary treatment of this waste, was still in the future.

The right wing New Democracy party was in power. In the face of objections to the scheme both by local residents and environmental campaigners, a tender for the treatment works had been launched by the state administration. The main opposition party, PASOK (Pan Hellenic Socialist Movement), sided with the objectors and made it a political issue in the general election of 1981.

When PASOK secured a majority and formed a new government, one of its first acts was to cancel the tender and to commission a new report on possible alternatives, including those that had been considered by Watsons but rejected. That report, drafted by a group from the National Technical University (NTU), proposed building a treatment works, not in close proximity to housing, but on a small uninhabited island some 1.5km offshore, the plant being designed to give secondary, i.e., biological treatment. Since the effluent would be treated to a much higher standard, the NTU group argued that it could be discharged through a short outfall that would cost less.

Non controversial, but an important component of the project, was to be a second trunk sewer from the city to relieve overloading of the existing trunk sewer.

Before proceeding with any new tenders, we had to address two key issues and give our recommendations, these being:

1. Was it technically feasible to construct an underwater conduit to take the waste across to the island, given the geological conditions and the presence of sewage sludge that had accumulated to a depth of more than a metre over the area?
2. How did the NTU proposal for secondary treatment with a short outfall compare with the original scheme of primary treatment coupled with a long sea outfall, in relation to environmental and public health outcomes?

There was much riding on our answers to these questions. It didn't take us too long to come to the conclusion that an inverted siphon across the narrows was technically feasible, and that it should be constructed with twin precast concrete pipes in a trench, in preference to a tunnel. Since that answer was one that our politically backed employers were happy to hear (the proponents of the onshore treatment scheme had cast doubt on its feasibility), that issue was settled, with the proviso that heavy inorganic solids that might otherwise settle out within the siphons should be removed in a preliminary treatment stage to be sited on the mainland.

Dealing with the primary treatment / long outfall *vs* secondary treatment/ short outfall debate was much more difficult however, since there were genuine advantages of the former scheme that the proponents of the latter were inclined to down play or counter with other disadvantages and risks. We fielded a leading authority in marine outfalls from California, Professor Norman Brooks, to wrestle with the problem and engage with the local academic group.

His clear analysis and his confidence in it enabled us to recommend that a primary treatment plant should be built on the island with the effluent being discharged through a long outfall farther out to sea in deep water, but that the works should be configured so as to facilitate the construction of a secondary treatment stage in the future. The rationale for this solution was complex and beyond the scope of this publication, but it did inform my choice of weekend swimming locations. EYDE accepted our findings and gave the green light.

The primary treatment and long outfall recommendation was sound at the time, since we were able to demonstrate that, without further treatment, the bacteriological standard of the EEC's Bathing Water Directive (76/160/EEC) would be met during the bathing season. Even if a secondary treatment plant was built in the future, which subsequently did prove to be necessary in the 1990s to comply with the Urban Wastewater Directive (91/271/EEC), the long outfall would continue to offer benefits over a short outfall.

There can be very few places in Greece that do not have some historic or archaeological significance and Psyttalia island is no exception. In the seas around that small island and towards the much larger island of Salamis to the west, a naval battle took place in 480 BC, in which, although outnumbered, the Greeks overcame the Persians. It was seen as a critical turning point in the Greco-Persian wars.

In more recent times, Psyttalia had been a naval prison and, like Alcatraz, a similar distance offshore from San Francisco, an escape to freedom involved a sea crossing. But there was an added constraint to any potential escapee from Psyttalia, the unattractive prospect of having to proceed through the grossly polluted waters between the island and the mainland.

When I landed on Psyttalia for the first time, the last prisoners had not long been evacuated, but left behind were the remnants of the guard dog pack and they were hungry. Our boatman knew of them and had brought some food, which kept them occupied while we had a good look around.

Client relations

For the first two or three months, the face of our client was Manolos Aftias, a political appointee who was one of a number of 'green guards', green being the colour of PASOK's emblem and posters. The green guards were enforcers, put into key positions to try to ensure that policy decisions made by the party and ratified by parliament were enacted as rapidly as possible and were not bogged down or obstructed by bureaucracy. It was a good working relationship, we had regular and productive working sessions, progress was being made and the first monthly fee invoices were processed and paid without any problem.

Aftias then informed us that EYDE could not continue as an outlier with the small team that was presently mobilised. He explained that, whilst he personally would continue to have technical oversight of the project, there would be a new director and administrative team that would be established within the regular state structure, authorised and able to launch tenders for the forthcoming large contracts. These would need to be administered in accordance with governmental protocols.

Mr Sfaellos was the director appointed and the relatively easygoing atmosphere that we had enjoyed initially became one of formality and distance. In our first few meetings I never saw him smile and it was clear that the way that we had been working until then was going to change. We had little alternative but to operate in a much more formal manner, which included justifying the need for the various personnel that we proposed to bring, all of whom had to be vetted. EYDE rigidly applied the fine print in our contract irrespective of any flexibility we were showing in the interest of what was needed for the job. Over a period of time however, although the administrative formalities remained unchanged, I believe that Mr Sfaellos did come round to trusting me, possibly when the first contract was awarded and he needed us firmly on side in dealings with the contractor.

Under the terms of our contract, we were paid by the month or part month for our personnel who were working in the EYDE office. All back-up provided at our home offices was deemed to be covered by the rates charged for the designated personnel. There were three grades, in ascending order of billed rates – Junior Specialist, Senior Specialist and Foreign Expert. A Junior Specialist had to have not less than five years of relevant experience post qualification and the Senior Specialist ten.

It could not be written into the contract as such, but we all understood that the rate for Junior grade applied to Greek engineers on the team, irrespective of their length of experience, as they would be on a lower salary even on a like for like basis. Senior grade applied to the expatriate engineers like me who were on a higher salary and had travel and local accommodation and subsistence costs to be covered within the billed rate. Travel days were not paid, except that if one left Athens on an afternoon flight, attendance at the office for that morning would be counted.

Foreign Experts were a special breed, billed at a rate two and a half times that of the Senior Specialist. We naively lined up some quite senior people in the industry to have short term inputs on the project, only to be told that either they didn't qualify as Experts, or that the task didn't demand one. From our side we needed to achieve the full number of Foreign Expert days that were in the contract, as there was a decent margin of profit in those, whereas from EYDE's side they sought to minimise them and use the unspent amount to increase the inputs of the Junior and Senior Specialists, whilst still keeping within the overall contract budget.

It was with some trepidation that Mr Gofas and I would go to Mr Sfaellos if we wished to propose the assignment of a Foreign Expert. Woodward Clyde lost out badly in these negotiations as they had envisaged that several senior people who they planned to bring from the US would be billable at the highest rate, in the event we only managed to get two Americans so graded. Haiste perceived the contract as a prestigious one that was good for the company image, it being accepted that the commission was only a modest earner, just above the minimum deemed to be financially worthwhile. For Woodward Clyde however, it turned out to be a loss making commission that they would have preferred not to have won.

Team working

EYDE did not want the consultant to provide services in the traditional manner. Although we had overall responsibility for the preparation of reports and tender documents, we were required to work as a team with EYDE personnel who would benefit from that collaborative working. Each regular member of our team was deemed to have a counterpart, and in my case I had two – Yiannis Tselentis and Nikos Kartsonas, two young and keen engineers who had been picked by Aftias and were a pleasure to work with. Yiannis was on top of all matters hydraulic and at least the equal of me in that regard. Nikos was the sewage treatment specialist and had the advantage over me of a relevant masters degree from a German university. However I was able to hold my own with him on primary treatment as I made it my business to make a thorough a study of that subject which was essential to our project.

Turning the hydraulic and process designs that lay at the heart of the project into practical realisation, through technical specifications and contractual documents for procurement, was where I could make a worthwhile contribution and it was clearly down to me to take the lead, but it was never an easy ride. When I offered an opinion on what I thought was the best way of dealing with a particular matter, I would often be putting forward what for me was just conventional wisdom and standard practice, but if I was challenged to justify and explain it that was something else. It meant going back to basics and justifying it to myself in the first instance. It was a healthy and stimulating discourse that had a beneficial effect on the quality of the tender documents which we prepared.

Other members of our team were not so fortunate with their counterparts. 'Gentleman Jim' Powers was from Houston, Texas, and he had the job of drafting tender documents for the twin pipe inverted siphon between Akrokeramos and Psyttalia. Unlike Yiannis and Nikos, who had been recruited for the duration of the project and were not permanent civil servants, Ms Belba was a long serving state employee. She was intimately familiar with the many regulations that applied to procuring public works in Greece, for her they were cast in tablets of stone and she did not wish to engage in debate about their appropriateness in relation to the particular requirements of our project. Meetings held to try to resolve matters could be heated, she had a somewhat strident voice that could penetrate all corners of the building when exercised to its full volume. "That screech owl[16]" was Jim's epithet.

Adrian Pyrah made the same transfer as I did from Baghdad to Athens, later becoming resident in the city with his wife and son. His mechanical engineering counterpart was Maria Koutmani, a fashionably dressed lady in her 40s with a bright and mildly coquettish personality. Adrian, I recall, bore the brunt of the workload of that section, but that of course was the rationale for our appointment.

To support Adrian, specialist electrical engineering advice on high voltage matters and communication technologies was on hand from visiting engineers, such as Murray Bolser. Murray was older than the rest of us but still full of ideas. One of them was an alternative measure of personal wealth that didn't rely on the fluctuations of the currency markets. Simply count of the number of electric motors at one's personal command he suggested. One should ensure not to overlook the smaller and hidden drives, such as those in an audio cassette player (two of them in tape to tape copying kit!); think of a basic car with wind down windows against a more expensive model with electric windows, intermediates with electric on the front only, pull up aerial or electric. The list is extensive, an interesting measure that could sit alongside the well known Big Mac Index.

The joint venture fit between Haiste and Woodward Clyde was a good one. We had competence in sewerage and sewage treatment, they had the track record in both marine outfalls and geotechnical engineering. The latter was important not just because of the pipeline crossing between the mainland and Psyttalia island, but there was 7km of trunk sewer to be constructed, mostly in rock tunnel.

Woodward Clyde's first engineer on the project was a geotechnical specialist who had worked on the San Francisco outfall. Don Treadwell was an impressive man, both in technical expertise and stature. "These hands have held moon rock" he declared in a meeting on one occasion to emphasise a particular point. It was true, he had been employed as a geotechnical engineer on the NASA lunar exploration programme. Bureaucratic niceties did not interest him greatly but would never get under his skin. I looked forward to his visits as he had an American 'can do' approach to the tasks in hand.

We had another Don on the team, Don Cargill from Bostock Hill and Rigby, a scientific consultancy based in Birmingham. We collaborated with them regularly when we needed analytical and advisory services in relation to industrial wastes. Don C took charge of updating the industrial waste survey and analyses that had been done by Watsons several years previously, and with Teddie Drew also on board we advised EYDE on industrial waste control policy. Strictly speaking this was the function of the Athens Water and Sewerage Company, EYDAP, but in the early years they kept their distance from the project, even though eventually they would be responsible for its operation and maintenance.

Mr Gofas had a two bedroom apartment in Kolonaki ('little colony'), a fashionable central district of Athens. It had been acquired for the use of his son, Christos, but as he was working overseas at the time we had the use of it for a while, being my home from home for many months. Other staff generally stayed in hotels and so eating out together every evening was the norm. In the 1980s, and well before the introduction of the euro, it was possible to have a taverna meal with drinks at roughly a third the price of an average meal out in the UK.

We all tended to have our favourites and we would ring the changes. 'Little Don's' was a small semi-basement establishment that opened out onto a main pedestrian way leading into Plaka, then as now a maze of souvenir shops, bars and restaurants clustered below the Parthenon. Simple fare was the order of the day, there was no menu, the proprietor would welcome us and let us know what he had cooked – we could go into his kitchen and have a look for ourselves. When it was time to pay he would lick his stubby pencil and tot up on a small pad, then round the total down to the nearest 50 drachmas. We were regulars and that entitled us to preferential terms. Tipping in tavernas (as opposed to restaurants) was extremely modest then, a few coins left at the end.

We tended to avoid Little Don's place when 'Big Don' was in town, as the rudimentary seating there didn't suit the latter's frame. Big Don's preference, which we saved for special occasions as it invariably exceeded our daily subsistence allowance, was the bar restaurant of the Grande Bretagne Hotel, with its soft leather button-back seating arranged in alcove style. Situated opposite the Greek parliament on Syntagma Square, it was the place to stay for visiting dignitaries, wealthy travellers and businessmen. There was a Hilton but it could never match the style and ambience of the Grand Bretagne. From time to time Don would treat us by producing his Woodward Clyde American Express card: "I'll put it on the marketing budget".

Once we had settled the big issue of the treatment plant location and outfall, Don Treadwell withdrew from the team and settled back to professional life in California. His replacement as geotechnical specialist to oversee the core drilling investigations and production of tender documents for the trunk sewer tunnel, was Ralph Fasano, a New Yorker of Italian roots. His lower travel cost and non billable time from the US east coast was an added advantage for Woodward Clyde.

For a time Ralph occupied the second bedroom in Mr Gofas's apartment, again keeping costs down. There was seven hours time difference with New York and on one occasion I remember being woken from my sleep in the early hours, hearing one side of a heated argument on the telephone. It went on for some time and I couldn't help picking up bits of it: "Let me speak to your mother!" I enquired gently the next day to learn that his son Charlie, coming into adolescence, had had an ear pierced, to the strong disapproval of his parents, Ralph either blaming himself or being blamed by his wife for not being at home to have prevented it.

As with any large and complex infrastructure project, a large amount of documentation was produced, doubled up by having to be in both Greek and English, since there was funding from the European Commission (EC) and it had to be open to bidders from all EEC countries on an equal level. However our tenders pre-dated the EC's introduction of its own procurement procedures that later became mandatory in the form of the so called Practical Guide. It impresses me still that every page of those documents was typed by Mr Gofas's secretary, Maria, in a small office perched on what looked to me to be a most uncomfortable high chair, in front of her IBM golf ball typewriter, sustained by cups of black coffee and an ever present cigarette.

The Greek editions of the documents were contractually binding and in the event of conflict would take precedence over the English. One bidder gave us some amusement resulting from the employment of a translator who was lacking in familiarity with the terminology. It was with some interest that we received their little boat (i.e. tender) documents.

Construction of the Greater Athens Project

One of my first tasks was to draw up a programme for the execution of the project showing the several stages through to final completion and handover. It was obvious that the earliest date for completion of the whole project would be a function of the time taken to complete the sewage treatment works, which was on the critical path, so I recommended that we give priority to this component and tender it first, while continuing with work on the other elements that could follow on sequentially. So as not to overload the EYDE administration, I arranged the programme such that, at any time, only one was at tender and contract award stage. However what was logical planning to me did not take account of the political dimension.

The PASOK government was conscious of the action that it took on coming into power, immediately stopping the project in the form favoured by the outgoing administration. More than two years had passed since they came to power in 1981, so although another general election was still some time away, this was politics and one could not predict the course of events. We were instructed to revise the programme by shifting the priority to the launch of tenders for the inverted siphon pipeline connecting the mainland with Psyttalia island. Notwithstanding the technical challenge in its construction, as a tender package it could be prepared in much shorter timescale than the treatment works. Once a contract was awarded for this component and construction got under way, the die was effectively cast for PASOK's favoured technical solution, minimising the chance of a reversion to the original scheme in the event of another change of government. Technically and financially it didn't make any sense to build a major asset and then for it to be mothballed for a couple of years, but politically it was a different matter.

The first tenders that we received for the inverted siphon component came in within the estimate and, after evaluating the bids, the contract was awarded to local contactor Athena SA. The huge precast concrete pipes were manufactured adjacent to the job site, on the land that had originally been allocated for the cancelled sewage treatment works. The joints between pipes were of the 'spigot and socket' type, but instead of the usual single rubber ring seal there were two rings with an annular space between. In conventional pipelaying practice on land there is a hydraulic test on completion of the whole line or in multi pipe sections, our underwater pipeline was tested for integrity after each joint was made, by applying a pressure test to the annulus between the two rubber rings.

There had been considerable uncertainty about the removal of the thick layer of sludge that lay on top of the sea bed along the route of the pipeline. That the material could be physically removed wasn't in any doubt, but would the volume taken out simply be replaced by an equivalent amount that would flow back into the trench from the sides? It was difficult to predict, but in the event we, and the contractor, were fortunate that a broad channel that was excavated through the sludge held firm and further excavation down into the bed rock could proceed, albeit in very murky conditions. The divers, who had to manoeuvre the pipe sections into place and make the joints, worked in extremely limited visibility.

For various reasons, tender documents for the treatment plant were not ready for issue until 1987. A few years previously, the NTU had carried out pilot plant trials on Athens wastewater. Valuable data had been obtained, demonstrating how both temperature (varying over the course of a year) and surface loading affected the rate of removal of suspended solids (SS) and biological oxygen demand (BOD) in a primary settlement tank. With the results of these trials available to bidders, in inviting them to propose tank sizes we would simply be testing the extent to which they were prepared to take a risk on meeting the process guarantee. Furthermore, there was no regulatory standard for primary settled effluent, nor was it critical to the performance of the marine outfall to hit a particular value, it was good enough if more than half of the suspended solids had been removed and with it a significant portion of the BOD.

If there was to be a future phase of secondary biological treatment, which with the passage of time was looking to be more likely, I knew that it could be optimised satisfactorily when preceded by a relatively high loading on the primary stage. EYDE agreed to my proposal that we fix the total surface area and volume of the primary tanks accordingly, based on the NTU results. It still left tenderers plenty of scope for developing their own cost effective designs around those core parameters.

Tendering for the treatment plant contract was competitive. There was no pre-qualification, eleven bids were received from Greek, British, Cypriot, French, German, Italian and Polish companies, the majority being joint venture partnerships.

As well as technical proposals and drawings, EYDE had decided that bidders should submit physical 3D models of their proposed design. On the day of tender submission, the office began to fill up with boxes containing the paper documents and we struggled to find sufficient table space to accommodate all of the models. My office on the first floor had a balcony overlooking the street and on hearing some commotion I looked out to see a small truck stopped outside, blocking the traffic. Two men were offloading the biggest model of them all; it was too large to fit in the lift or to negotiate up the stairs, so it was propped up against a wall in the lobby, where it remained for many months, gathering dust. Perhaps visiting politicians and others gained something from viewing the models, but they didn't play any significant part in the tender evaluation, which was conducted on the basis of the technical documents and drawings. I felt that bidders had enough to have to do without adding to their workload for no real benefit.

The award of a contract for the construction of the sewage treatment works marked a change in my role on the project. The job demanded both a civil and mechanical engineer to work full time with EYDE in the review and approvals of the contractor's designs, and then to support their supervising engineers during construction. Although the Athens project had predominated, I was still involved with other projects in the UK and elsewhere and was disinclined to dedicate myself to a single project, however prestigious and technically interesting. My wife had a good job and a social circle of friends and would not have come out to Athens to live there. Clive Taylor, who had been working in Libya for consulting engineer Howard Humphries, joined us as resident project manager. I was promoted to become a director of Haiste International Ltd., as we were by then, and with it came responsibility for client and JV partner relationships. I continued to make frequent visits to Athens in that capacity as well as for technical oversight and the preparation of key reports.

I hadn't been on Psyttalia for some time and construction had not long started when I went across there with Clive. It had been written into the specification that the plant should be built on the west side of the island and that the view from the east, visible from ships entering and leaving Piraeus harbour, should "maintain the historically important perspective". The contractor's drawings showed a compliant arrangement that left a narrow ridge between the plant and the eastern shore line. Unfortunately this constraint had not been relayed to the crew of the bulk excavating machinery and when I landed at the west harbour I was able to have a clear line of sight through to the Saronic Gulf and the shipping lanes to the east. Coaches and horses came to mind at that moment and I brought it up with the site agent, who could only say sorry, but the damage was done. The ridge could be reformed at a later stage, but it could never be brought back to its original natural craggy slope. A few years later that condition was quietly dropped when a secondary biological treatment plant was planned, as we needed every square metre of the island to squeeze in the vast expanse of aeration and secondary settlement tanks.

Of the many incidents during construction, one that is memorable connected two brothers some 3,500 km apart. Waste from the city discharges from the trunk sewer at sea level. Flows have to be elevated by several metres to be able to pass downstream by gravity through the inverted siphon, treatment works and marine outfall. Originally devised by Archimedes, screw pumps are ideal for this duty and the Dutch, who use them extensively in the drainage of polders, were at the forefront of the 20th century versions.

The huge 3.4m diameter screws were manufactured in the Netherlands and then transported by ship to our site. They were lashed to the decks of cargo vessels, but in December 1989 one of the consignments encountered rough seas in the Bay of Biscay. One screw broke loose and rolled off the deck and into the sea. The captain wrote in his log that the screw sank, but that didn't ring true to us as the central shaft was a hollow tube sealed at both ends. Unless the tube had become punctured it should float, albeit low in the water with only the top of the flights visible, and a danger to shipping.

Several weeks later I was alerted by a newspaper report with a photograph showing the huge screw, which had washed up onto a beach in Port Talbot, South Wales. I contacted Clive to let him know. "I have news for you" I said, and told him about the discovery. "In that case I also have news for you, my brother is the Director of Works for Neath Council" was his reply! Ken Taylor was on the scene shortly afterwards and reported to us on its condition, which was surprisingly good. A local resident had attempted to tether it with a rope and claim salvage, but on the next tide it moved again and landed on some rocks, causing more significant damage. The pump's manufacturer made an inspection and declared it to be written off, so it was towed away for scrap.

An ancient culvert

I fielded many queries while working in the EYDE office, not all of them connected with our project. I didn't object to being diverted from the job in hand occasionally and to spend a bit of time on something unrelated.

Another ministry department was overseeing the extension of the Metamorphosis wastewater treatment plant and it had been alerted to the possibility of a very old culvert crossing the site, at considerable depth. There was a concern that the culvert might be below one of the aeration tanks, which was designed with a piled foundation, risking a pile penetrating into it. Could I suggest the best means of establishing its route?

After a discussion on available modern methods, I casually mentioned that, before those became available, an earlier generation might have tried dowsing. No one in the office had heard of it and I explained how it was done. Inevitably that led to a demand for a field demonstration, which I agreed to do on condition that as few people as possible were around and that whatever was revealed would not be relied upon as a substitute for the use of current technology. So the following weekend I turned up at the site, fence wire rods made up, and proceeded to give it a go.

When using the rods, their reaction is a function of the depth of the discontinuity that is being detected. A shallow item triggers the reaction when you are nearly over it. At greater depth the reaction starts some distance away. I picked up something which seemed to be as much as 10m below ground, its route skirting the corner where one of the tanks was to be constructed. That done and witnessed by the few onlookers, I took my leave. They were not going to get anything in writing from me, but I was prepared to say that the report of a deep culvert under the site in the vicinity of the proposed tanks could be correct, and that further investigations should be undertaken.

Back in the office on Monday there was plenty of chatter about the experience and various people wanted to have a try, resulting in much amusement.

Other endeavours in Greece

In Greece there was no shortage of well established and competent consulting engineers, and Greek contractors were undertaking major works beyond the country's boundaries. It was unrealistic for us to think that we could simply pick up standard commissions on the basis of our presence on the Athens project, which was a bit of a special. However we did get appointed to provide technical support to the Ministry of Environment on the wastewater treatment plant for Thessaloniki, Greece's second city in the north. Adrian Pyrah became our man in residence, moving there with his family from Athens, I and other specialists provided part time input in regular visits.

Apart from the Athens project, Mr Gofas was content to remain focused on his dams and irrigation work and was not especially interested to explore other potential opportunities. With his acquiescence therefore I did the rounds of a number of other local consultants, with mixed reaction and only one small contract resulting.

For civil servants the working day comprised one long session from 07.30 to 14.30, a coffee break and a mid day sandwich would be taken at the desk. A private sector office typically opened up a bit later in the morning and worked through into the early evening but with a long break for lunch in mid afternoon. It meant that, if they so desired, those working for the state had time available to supplement their income, either as sole traders or working in a private sector office in the afternoon-evening session. An evening meal wouldn't commence until after nine at the very earliest, anything before that was strictly for tourists.

Yiannis Tselentis and Nikos Kartsonas were practitioners of the doubled-up working day model, they were keen and reached the point when, together with a colleague who worked in highways, they were ready to form their own company, which they named Nama. They revealed this to me before the official launch and we discussed their aspirations and business plans. By this time Haiste had been taken over by Danish consultants, Carl Bro, and I introduced Nama to them. It led to a collaborative arrangement and a whole new area of work for me and for Carl Bro over the next fifteen years.

Yiannis and Nikos complemented one another well. Yiannis was full of brio and ideas would flow from him fast and furious. Nikos had a steadier approach and would think things through carefully before expressing a view, although that apparent reticence may just have been due to the fact that English was his third language after Greek and German and his needing some additional time to deliver his thoughts in my native tongue. (It embarrasses me that I could barely manage the simplest of conversations in my schoolboy French and my Greek never progressed beyond basic greetings, dialogue with taxi drivers and ordering food and drink in a taverna).

My abiding image of Yiannis is being with him in the Nama office meeting room during our regular evening sessions, his spending lengthy periods of time on his mobile telephone, at the desk or pacing up and down. Not long after I had concluded the assignments in Greece, I was deeply saddened to learn that he had died from a brain tumour, a young man of around 40 years of age. Nikos put it down to the phone that was clamped to his ear, day in day out, for many hours.

At the weekends

If you overlook the city from a viewpoint to the north, unless the wind is from that direction, it will be apparent immediately that the downtown area is nestled under a blanket of photochemical smog, the 'nefos', the result of the products of fossil fuel combustion, ozone and a series of chemical reactions driven by sunlight. Living and working in the city centre one didn't give it much thought, nothing could be done about it anyway, but at the weekend a trip out of the city offered the opportunity to breathe noticeably cleaner air, quite apart from getting around and visiting the many attractions that that country has to offer. It gave the lungs a chance to recover from the abuse which you had imposed upon them.

The coastline settlements to the south of the city were readily accessible for a day trip or overnight stay, as were the Saronic Gulf islands, a short journey from Piraeus by Russian built hydrofoil. During the winter months a three hour drive from Athens took us to Mount Parnassos and its skiing facilities. The state owned airline, Olympic Airways, provided low cost heavily subsidised flights to the islands, the government's rationale being the desire to prevent population decline in their border facing territories, especially those within sight of Turkey's mainland.

In June 1985 there was another general election and the Greek citizens exercised their democratic right with enthusiasm, after all their forefathers invented the concept (democracy literally meaning rule by people). Adrian and I decided that, at the election weekend (the vote is held on Sunday), we would make a trip to ancient Olympia, on the west coast of the Peloponnese. On the Saturday we set off early in the car, only to become trapped in a long queue of crawling traffic heading out of the city on the main highway. We had failed to take account of the peculiarities of the Greek electoral roll – very many Athenians retain a property or residential qualification in the provincial town or village of their ancestral origins, their vote is registered there and not in their main city dwelling.

After some hours, eventually we crossed the Corinth Canal and traffic started to move a little faster, but by this time it was mid afternoon and we had still to find accommodation, so we decided to call a halt at the village of Diakofto on the shore of the Gulf of Corinth, where we found a pension with rooms available. We had stumbled upon the sea level end of the Diakofto to Kalavrita mountain railway, a spectacular narrow gauge line that winds its way through the Vouraikos gorge. Considered an engineering feat in its time, rack and pinion drive is used on the steepest sections of the track which rises a total of 750m. Kalavrita is an attractive tourist destination now, but was the site of one of the German military's worst reprisals against the general population, after Greek resistance forces had killed 78 soldiers of the Third Reich. All men over 16 years of age were taken and shot, more than 500 died.

The 1985 election saw PASOK retaining power, so our politicised project remained on track.

10 Water Distribution Network Management and Water Conservation

'SPRINT'

It was obvious that there was little point in pursuing traditional consultancy commissions in Greece, we needed to bring services that were new to that market. In the UK we had developed competence and a track record in the computer analysis of water distribution networks. In parallel we had developed expertise in various aspects of asset management including leakage control and rehabilitation of pipelines. I had discussed this a few times with Yiannis Tselentis and he could see the need for it in Greece, but how were we to bring it to fruition? Infrastructure projects in Greece went from conception to realisation in a series of formal stages that were laid down in public procurement regulations. Clients and consultants were geared up to the delivery of services under that model, but it was inappropriate to the types of services that we had in mind. A couple of the municipally owned Greek water companies had been approached, but it was a novel concept and they had no procedure for it.

In his office one day Yiannis handed me some information that he had obtained about an EC programme, "SPRINT", launched by their technology and innovation directorate, DGXIII. Funding was available for "technology transfer" projects, such transfers being between countries and organisations, and/or between one industry and another. It looked to be the way in for us, since the prospect of getting funding from the EC would concentrate minds. If that meant coming up with a new model under which they could acquire both external services and new skills for their personnel, then perhaps clients might be open to it.

A SPRINT project had three stages – Definition, Implementation, and Dissemination. To get started it was enough to come up with a basic idea and a consortium of partners, from more than one country of the EEC (as it was then). If selected, funding would then be granted for the Definition Phase under which a detailed and costed plan would be developed. We were required to use Goal Orientated Project Planning (GOPP, or ZOPP in the original German), and Logical Framework Analysis (LFA). This was my introduction to many new terms beloved of the EEC bureaucracy that had to be learned and used in the presentation of our proposal, pitched to an adjudication panel.

DGXIII were keen that the project was a real partnership of the participants, albeit with a lead partner and overall project manager, which was Haiste-Carl Bro. It was cemented in a workshop in Luxembourg attended by all of the proposed partners, with our DGXIII manager, Tony Boylan, acting as facilitator. A key objective of the workshop was to agree upon the Logical Framework and the first step of that was to arrive at a consensus on what was perceived to be the Core Problem that was to be solved. Eventually we settled on: "Unaccounted for Water[17] is excessive in EEC member states", which then led logically to scoping the project so as to tackle the identified causes and the development of a project plan with its inputs, outputs, verifiable indicators etc.

It's easy to be scathing of the seemingly tortuous procedures, form filling, box ticking, jargon etc., beloved of bureaucrats everywhere, but I was won over by Logical Framework Analysis and was happy to deploy it on several projects subsequently. On projects funded by the EC and other development agencies it was obligatory, and whilst some may have regarded it as just another hurdle to be jumped, I found it to be genuinely useful and became a convert. It stood me in good stead when, in the late period of my career, I obtained a number of commissions assisting mainstream consulting firms in preparing bids for new work.

Our first willing partners were the Greek municipal water undertakings of Larissa and Thiva, the latter now a small town and backwater that had once been the ancient and powerful city of Thebes, they were DEYAL and DEYATh respectively. Whilst we, Haiste-Carl Bro, would transfer technology to both Nama and the DEYAs, we invited Yorkshire Water to join us as a second UK partner, to bring the operational and customer facing experience to the project that we did not have. To comply with the

Mausoleum of the 10th Duke of Hamilton, Hamilton.
© *South Lanarkshire Museum Service*

Red Road flats under construction, Glasgow, c1963.
© *Herald and Times Group, Glasgow*

Graduation photograph, Glasgow, 1967

An open sewer in a poor district of Baghdad. The picture was taken by the author in 1975 but similar scenes witnessed by the author when he visited in 1998 on assignment for the UN during 'weapons of mass destruction' sanctions regime.

"thiobacillus concretivorus" Front cover of New Civil Engineer,
19th February 1976.
© *Emap Publishing Ltd.*

Inspecting corrosion inside Baghdad's east bank trunk sewer, Baghdad, 1977. Left: David Knight (Bostock Hill & Rigby), right: Ian Aldred (Haiste).

Author meets trucks arrived from Dubai with GRP pipes for lining trunk sewers, Baghdad, 1979.

Laying of 3 metre diameter precast concrete trunk sewer, also served as occasional air raid shelter, Baghdad, 1980.

Construction of trunk sewer, traditional in-situ concrete design, Baghdad, 1980. In shot left: Bernard Eagles (Haiste), right: Nabil Awad (Baroudi Awad).

Kerkh (west bank) Sewage Treatment Works, under construction, Baghdad, 1982.
Photograph by David Noakes

Garden of New British Club, Baghdad, 1975.
From Ambler family archive

Haiste directors with Lord Lieutenant of Yorkshire on occasion of receiving a Queen's Award for Export, Leeds, 1982.
Photographer unknown

Wastewater from c 3m population discharging without treatment into Saronic Gulf, Akrokeramos, Athens, 1983.

Sea bed sludge being removed along route of inverted siphon from mainland to Wastewater treatment plant on Psyttalia island, Athens, 1985.

Undersea pipeline laying, Akrokeramos – Psyttalia, Athens, 1986.

Physical models of hydraulic structures of Athens Wastewater Treatment Plant. Front to rear: Yiannis Tselentis (EYDE), Clive Taylor (Carl Bro Haiste), Professor of Civil Engineering, Thessaloniki, Greece, 1989.

Greater Athens Wastewater Treatment Plant, under construction, settlement tanks and outfall pipeline manufacture, Psyttalia, Athens, c1990.

Archimedean screw intended for main inlet pumping station at Athens wastewater treatment plant, lost at sea then found washed up on Morpha beach, Port Talbot, Wales, January 1990.

Haiste Group management conference c1986, (predominantly white male!). Delegates mentioned in the book: Geoff Bowyer (top row C), the author (top row R), David Keegan (2nd row L), John Haiste (4th row L), David Noakes (6th row R), Ken McDougall (7th row left), Ian Ramsden (behind front row L), Derek Williams (front row 2nd from R), Harvey Roberts (front row R).

UNRWA headquarters, Gaza City, 1993

Emptying household latrine, Rafah, Gaza, 1993.
Dean Guesmia (Carl Bro) and Bill Hoadley (UNRWA) observing.

Author with Mayors of Leeds, Thiva and Larissa (Greece), Leeds, 1993.
BKW Public Relations, Leeds

Yiannis Tselentis (centre) with his Nama SPRINT team and DEYAL personnel, Larissa, Greece, 1994.

SPRINT project Open Day and partners workshop, Larissa, Greece, 1994. Left to right: Ian Paterson (Carl Bro Haiste), Ed Dunlop (Local Government Computer Services Board, Ireland), Dr Reiner Wohlgemuth (Stadtwerke Chemnitz, Germany), Alex Gilmour (Carl Bro Haiste), Tony Kearon (Dundalk, Ireland) Yiannis Tselentis (Nama).

DEYAL staff receiving certificates of completion of training by Yorkshire Water and Carl Bro, Leeds, 1994. Left to right: the author, Costas Papandreou, Dina Kyrakopolou, Christos Vatsis.
BKW Public Relations, Leeds

Κυκλοφορεί σήμερα Κυριακή ο «Reporter» μαζί με την «ΕΛΕΥΘΕΡΙΑ»

ΕΛΕΥΘΕΡΙΑ

ΙΔΡΥΤΗΣ: Γ. Β. ΔΗΜΗΤΡΑΚΟΠΟΥΛΟΣ — Η ΑΡΧΑΙΟΤΕΡΗ ΚΑΘΗΜΕΡΙΝΗ ΕΦΗΜΕΡΙΔΑ ΤΗΣ ΛΑΡΙΣΑΣ

ΦΥΛΑΚΕΣ ΛΑΡΙΣΑΣ: Οι κρατούμενοι τις παρέδωσαν χθες στον Περιφερειάρχη Θεσσαλίας

Ματαιώθηκε μεγάλη απόδραση...

* Ως την τελευταία στιγμή οι στασιαστές έσκαβαν σήραγγα άψογης κατασκευής σε βάθος 4 μέτρων!
* Τεράστιες οι ζημιές που προκλήθηκαν στον βασικό εξοπλισμό των φυλακών

Ρεπορτάζ
Ευ. Ρηγόπουλος
Φωτο: Σπ. Τσαντόπουλος

Στα χέρια της πολιτείας και των φυλάκων τους βρίσκονται από χθες οι δικαστικές φυλακές Λάρισας, μετά από κατάληψη διαρκείας πέντε ημερών από τους 660 κρατουμένους.

Το γεγονός ανακοινώθηκε επίσημα το μεσημέρι σε κοινή συνέντευξη τύπου των εκπροσώπων της πολιτείας και των κρατουμένων, που έγινε σε χώρο της φυλακής.

Προηγουμένως όμως και συγκεκριμένα γύρω στις 4 τα ξημερώματα αποκαλύφθηκε η ύπαρξη σήραγγας, ακριβώς στο σημείο που υποψιάζονταν οι αρχές, «αριστούργημα» κατασκευής. Ηταν στην πλευρά του τοίχου προς την κατεύθυνση της Καρδίτσας, όπου την προηγούμενη είχε σκαφτεί τάφρος βάθους τεσσάρων μέτρων.

Η αποκάλυψη έγινε όταν οι δυνάμεις των ΜΑΤ που φύλαγαν απ'

ο υποψήφιος δραπέτης υποχώρησε στο εσωτερικό της σήραγγας. Ακολούθησε η ρίψη δακρυγόνων στην σήραγγα ώστε να εμποδιστεί κάθε νέα προσπάθεια απόδρασης.

Η ΠΑΡΑΔΟΣΗ

Γύρω στις 10 το πρωί άρχισε η παράδοση των φυλακών, με τους κρατούμενους να μπαίνουν στα κελιά τους και τον περιφερειάρχη κ. Νικ. Ζαμπουνίδη, καθώς και τον διευθυντή των φυλακών κ. Κων. Τσουρέλη, σε χρέη δεσμοφύλακα να τους κλειδώνουν, σύμφωνα με την προηγηθείσα συμφωνία.

Αρχικά, φάνηκε ότι υπήρχε κάποια διαφωνία, επειδή στις επαφές που γίνονταν και με άλλες φυλακές της χώρας (Πάτρα, Κέρκυρα) οι εκεί κρατούμενοι αντέδρασαν. Σαν λόγο προέβαλαν ότι κατά την διάρκεια της νύχτας εξυβρί-

Συνέχεια στην 8η σελίδα

Ο γ.γ. Περιφέρειας και οι αστυνομικές αρχές στη χθεσινή συνέντευξη, παρουσία

SPRINT project front page news in Ελευθερία [Eleftheria]: gaol inmates captured by police after their tunnel was discovered by DEYAL's leak detection team, Larissa, Greece, March 1996
Ελευθερία

Head of Karl Marx in front of former Communist Party headquarters, Chemnitz (the city during the Soviet era being known as Karlmarkstadt),1995.

Cork Corporation Water Department technicians listening for leaks, Cork, Ireland, 1998.

Trenčín Right Bank Wastewater Treatment Plant, Slovakia, 2004.

Trenčín Right Bank WWTP, author hands copy of the plant's Final Completion Certificate to asset owner TVK's Project Manager, Monika Čižnárová, Trenčín, Slovakia, December 2004.

Nitra Wastewater Treatment Plant nearing completion of construction, Nitra, Slovakia, 2005.

Crystal clear treated effluent from Nitra WWTP, Nitra 2007.

SPRINT criteria we needed another partner from a third EEC country and, through some contacts that I can no longer recall, we were very fortunate that a real heavyweight in the business, Canal de Isabel, the water undertaking for Madrid, agreed to join us.

Getting the Greek municipalities on board was not straightforward and during that process we invited them to Leeds for discussions and meetings with us and with Yorkshire Water. Expecting their representatives to be the chief engineers of the water companies whom we had met, we were surprised to learn that their respective town mayors were going to be with them. It put a new dimension on the visit.

I contacted the office of the Leeds mayor and explained that we were having this visit, and could our Greek mayors meet the Lord Mayor of Leeds? I was pleased that the Leeds mayor at that time, Councillor Denise Atkinson, was agreeable, and so we met in the Mayor's Parlour of Leeds's impressive Victorian Town Hall. Small gifts or mementos were exchanged in the traditional custom. Ms Atkinson was known for her unconventional style of dress, which rather surprised our visitors in their formal suits. The commemorative photograph taken outside the Guildhall was more colourful as a result.

In volume terms, a small leak that goes undiscovered for a long time can lose more water than a large one that becomes apparent immediately, gets reported and fixed quickly. The fundamental objective of 'active leakage control' is to minimise the time that elapses between a leak occurring and its repair. I thought that we had got that message across at an early stage, but on a visit to Thiva we were taken to a valve house and inside it water could be seen escaping from a valve or joint. Naturally I mentioned it and was surprised that the response was: "It's alright, we know about it".

I was fortunate that we had engineers in our Leeds office who were extremely competent in hydraulic modelling and its practical applications and they were interested to work with me on this new endeavour. UK section heads did not always look favourably on the international department, since they perceived that their best staff and key members of their project teams could be pulled out to service an international project, to the detriment of their domestic work. The staff themselves often looked at it differently however. Senior graduate engineers Alex Gilmour and

Rosie Richmond were keen and welcomed the increased responsibility that was entailed when they were placed into our partner offices and were perceived, rightly, as the "experts". They both excelled too in being hands-on trainers of the partner personnel. Their section leader, Ian Paterson, was prepared to give it his best shot and the whole team gelled as a result.

DEYAL staff embraced the project enthusiastically and appreciated the opportunity of working with us and with Yorkshire Water, who put on a training course in the UK and awarded certificates at the end of it. When the project was concluded, DEYAL had computerised their records, updated their metering and reduced their losses. It was a success.

Most people will be familiar with the sight of a leakage technician patrolling an area with a listening stick, using either the traditional wooden rod or the modern electronic variety. Other acoustic methods that are deployed to detect the sound of escaping water include ground microphones. At Larissa we had an unexpected project result with this equipment when, at night time on the street where the local prison is located, an unusual sound was heard. On further investigation the sound was identified as some of the prison's occupants digging their way out through a tunnel. This discovery and subsequent parading of the crestfallen escapees with their police captors was keenly picked up by media outlets. It was a further boost for our project and another opportunity to get our water conservation message across to the public.

Canal de Isabel's engineering managers regarded themselves as being up there with industry leaders. Nevertheless they recognised that, at that time, UK water companies and consultants were at the forefront in some respects and consequently they should participate in initiatives of the kind that we were promoting, especially if endorsed by an arm of the European Commission. Canal offered up three districts where they were facing problems and which were set up as pilot projects. The individual elements of our project were all in place within Canal, and were not new to them, but our systematic and holistic approach was, and that together with the opportunity to compare their practices with one of the leading UK water undertakings was one of the benefits. And we did reduce the losses in their pilot areas.

It did not go unnoticed in Luxembourg that SPRINT Specific Project 257 (SP 257) was successful. It led to DGXIII approaching us to take on another partner, the newly privatised water supply undertaking for the city of Chemnitz in Germany, in the former German Democratic (sic) Republic. Chemnitz was the city's historic name, but it had been renamed as Karlmarxstadt during the communist dictatorship. It reverted to Chemnitz after the fall of the Berlin wall.

Like neighbouring city Dresden, large areas of Chemnitz were destroyed in the allied bombing campaign of WWII. Much of the city centre had to be rebuilt and this was done in Soviet architectural style. The most prominent building facing the main square was the Communist party headquarters and in front of that, on a plinth, was a huge bronze of the head of Karl Marx. Behind the sculpture, extending to the full height of the external wall of the building, was a massive bronze plaque on which Marx's famous call for workers of the world to unite was declared in numerous languages. I wondered if this imagery might be due for removal, but I was informed that it was part of their history, albeit a dark part, and it was important that people should not forget its horrors.

I made my first visit to Chemnitz in 1995, so it was only six years since the end of the Soviet era. There were many reminders of the recent past, the most visible on an everyday basis being the numerous Trabant cars that scooted around the streets, leaving trails of blue two-stroke oil smoke. Stadtwerke Chemnitz booked me into the best hotel which, under new ownership, was in the process of being refurbished, but I had one of the original rooms which had decor and fittings that dated back to the early decades of the 20th century, it was basic but clean and had the essentials so it was fine for me. It would be nice to think that they preserved one room in that form for historic purposes.

Key staff and a director from Statdwerke Chemnitz came across to Leeds and followed the path trodden earlier by our Greek partners in visits and meetings, but fortunately the Chemnitz mayor didn't tag along so I didn't have to set up another municipal encounter. A highlight of their visit was an evening out at one of Joshua Tetley's traditional pubs, The Queen in Burley Road, which sadly now is a small Tesco store, followed by excellent Indian cuisine at the Corner Cafe opposite. It was a new experience for our guests.

Buoyed with the success of the SPRINT programme, DGXIII extended the funding on offer and, as well as initiating new projects, they encouraged existing successful projects like ours to expand. Dissemination of the results of our project was an obligatory component – we published a series of newsletters under the snappy title "Newsleak" and interested organisations were encouraged to participate as official observers. In the second phase the observers became full partners – in Ireland we were joined by the municipalities of County Meath and Dundalk town, and the Local Government Computer Services Board (LGCSB). In Portugal our new partners were the water company of Lisbon (EPAL) and the national laboratory of civil engineering (LNEC).

In Greece, the association of Greek municipal water companies, EDEYA, came on board. They were looking for a guidance manual that brought together the several strands of our approach – how and on what basis should a water undertaking carry out an assessment? What parameters should be used in evaluation and what should be the priorities for action? The manual that we produced for EDEYA in Greece paved the way for guidelines that we developed subsequently in Ireland and South Africa.

In 1994, part way through our project, Water Research in the UK published what became a seminal suite of documents under the title "Managing Leakage". Our project encapsulated many of the same principles, but we took a wider and holistic asset management approach.

SP257 concluded in 1996 and a professionally produced video was made as part of the Dissemination Phase. I was asked to give it a title and I settled on "Managing the Network, Not Just the Leakage".

I had spent 30 years being involved with schemes of works requiring capital expenditure, including some projects that represented engineering at a grand scale and which could grace the pages of a company brochure. Now I was dabbling in the small diameter pipe network and connections into individual properties. Not by any means the glamorous end of our business, but a vital part of delivering a reliable supply of drinking water to consumers. To me it offered no less of an intellectual challenge and there was real satisfaction when hard won outcomes were accomplished. With SPRINT coming to an end, I hoped for further opportunities, as I felt that there was scope to do more in forward planning of water services and in the rehabilitation of distribution networks.

Ireland

The SPRINT project had been well received in the Irish Republic where the supply of drinking water at that time was predominantly the responsibility of local authorities, as it had been in England and Wales until 1974 when regional water authorities were formed. The national picture was further complicated by the existence in rural areas of hundreds of so called Group Schemes that are, in effect, private networks, some having their own water source, others purchasing water from their municipality.

With the exception of Dublin, and to a lesser extent Cork, there was no general shortage of water in that famously green island. Much of it was deliverable to users at low cost. However consumption by commercial users was inadequately monitored, local authorities as well as group scheme trustees operated their distribution networks on a shoe string budget, and personnel were unfamiliar with and untrained in asset management and water loss control. It didn't help that unmetered domestic households that were supplied by their municipality were not charged, it being regarded by consumers as a service that should be provided free at the point of delivery and funded out of general taxation. The situation was one of massive losses and waste.

With the 'Celtic Tiger' bounding forward, resulting in a year on year steady increase in demand for water, the prospect of water shortages was real. Only Dublin Corporation, with an eye to how things were developing in the UK and being in a more critical supply-demand balance situation, had any systematic approach to the reduction of losses. The Irish Department of Environment and Local Government realised that business as usual was not an option and it embarked upon a programme of water conservation and network management projects, based upon the SPRINT model. They decreed that no new capital works to augment water supply would be funded unless steps had been taken to reduce losses.

The first of these post SPRINT water conservation projects brought together the cities of Galway in the west and Waterford in the south east. Having established a presence in the UK, Carl Bro had then gone on to acquire KML (the initials of its founder Kevin McLoughlin), a small but well respected structural engineering practice in Dublin, and we bid for the Galway and Waterford commission as KML Carl Bro. We agreed to go in with Ryan Hanley, a consulting firm from Galway with a track record in water supply, that sector being wholly absent from KML's portfolio.

It was my job to lead with the pitch to the interview panel which comprised a senior civil servant from the Department and the City Engineers of Galway and Waterford. It seemed to be going well enough until Galway's City Engineer, Tom Kilgarriff, asked me a question and I gave an answer he didn't much like, I sensed immediately that I had bombed when he came back with a follow up in rather confrontational manner. Somehow at that moment it occurred to me to quote Dennis Healey's famous First Law of Politics – "when you're in a hole stop digging". It lightened the mood and we survived the rest of the interview. That test passed we were then awarded the commission.

The Galway and Waterford commission was the first of a series of similar contracts that we were awarded in Ireland, in Counties Longford, Meath and Wexford, in the town of Clonmel and the city of Cork. The holistic approach that we had started under SPRINT was further developed in these projects and, in all of them, as well as achieving meaningful reductions in water losses, we delivered a Strategic Operational and Management Plan, known to all as the SOMP. In Waterford we also introduced to Ireland so called 'no-dig' methods of rehabilitation of pipe networks, using slip lining, pipe bursting and moling techniques. Our core team was again Ian Paterson, Alex Gilmour and Rosie Richmond, who transitioned from SPRINT to Ireland. Alex found love there and married a Waterford girl.

We recruited our first Irish water engineer, Brian McLoughlin, a Longford man and a true computer boffin, his skills lay in the melding of human biological and electronic brains, and this set him apart somewhat from the others. He was fascinated however by the water systems analysis spreadsheet which I had developed to do the water accounting and to produce key performance indicators, and we were able to get along.

There was a school of thought that prevailed, encapsulated in the phrase "the big leaks always find you". It had been quoted by a Dublin Corporation engineer in my presence. Mostly they do of course, but not always, and I was delighted when our joined up approach proved that there could be exceptions, as we knew. Rosie was our finder when trying to validate her computer model, she concluded that there had to be either an unknown source of demand (illicit connection) or a very large leak from one of the water mains. The search team was despatched and discovered a massive escape of water that was likely to have been running for months if not years. It was finding its way unseen into a surface water culvert and thence into a river. It was a good moment.

On the retirement of Kevin McLoughlin, KML Carl Bro became Carl Bro Ireland and moved from outdated premises in Terenure, where it occupied a converted house with temporary buildings in its back yard, to brand new purpose built accommodation in Dundrum. I was in charge of Carl Bro Ireland's water department and was successful for a time as we pressed home the technical and track record advantage that we had over the opposition in our specialist field, but it was much more difficult to obtain work in the traditional sphere of capital scheme development. To get work of that kind we needed an Irish national and local resident with relevant experience, someone who could be groomed to take over from me.

That recruitment was a struggle but finally we employed Liam, a senior engineer from a local authority. I was on friendly terms with his boss, I had tried to get work from him, although without success, and I thought that poaching one of his key staff would not go down too well. But Liam assured me that there would be no hard feelings and so we duly appointed him. He then revealed that his former boss had advised him that he could have his old job, or an equivalent, back if things didn't work out with us! It became obvious after a few months that Liam just wasn't cut out for life in the private consulting sector and as he had a Plan B it was by mutual consent that he took it. His replacement, Tom Cuddy, came to us from a competitor consulting firm and he knew the ropes, so when it came time for me to bow out there was a viable succession plan.

Carl Bro assigned a series of 'minders' from their Copenhagen office, to take care of everyday liaison and to ensure that we were properly integrated with the parent company in all relevant aspects. Our first was Max Metzlaff and he shook things up, it was bound to be thus in a take-over situation. When he left us there was a small ceremony when nice things were said, our MD, Steve Day, presented him with a polished wooden box and invited Max to open it. Inside was a hand grenade. For once Max was at a loss for words and was visibly taken aback, but after a pregnant pause and with the aid of a shot of Aquavit, or perhaps it was Gammel Dansk, he recovered his composure.

As we reached the millennium, Henrik was our latest minder. He made a visit to the Dublin office to meet the local directors and managers and to review the business generally. Naturally the subject of business development came up and he indicated that he expected me to follow up various opportunities in the environmental sector of which he was aware. That discussion was a key moment in shaping my remaining career in the years ahead. I was 58 years of age, I had done my share of management, including marketing and business development, and I had been moderately successful within my own sphere, but personal satisfaction was realised more readily by active participation in projects and I concluded that it was time to resign from my position as an operating company director and dip my toe in the freelance waters.

There were still projects which I had in Ireland that needed to be completed, so by mutual consent with Carl Bro management I saw them through to a satisfactory conclusion while exploring other opportunities, on the understanding that I wouldn't accept any employment that could give rise to a conflict of interest. In the event, although I obtained my first freelance assignment from one of Carl Bro's competitors within a relatively short time, other assignments were coming in from both Carl Bro UK and Denmark that I was offered and accepted. In the UK I had the chance to try my hand at expert witness work, and Copenhagen engaged me as a team leader and specialist for projects in Slovakia and South Africa.

South Africa

Much of Carl Bro International (CBI)'s workload came through the various international development agencies, such as the World, Asian and African Development Banks, and especially the Danish government's international aid agency, Danida (later Danced). In 2000, CBI was awarded a prestigious commission in South Africa, to support the Department of Water Affairs and Forestry (DWAF) in the implementation of key provisions of the new National Water Act. It was a visionary piece of legislation that had the ambitious and worthwhile aim of managing the water resources of the country for the benefit of all of its citizens, as well as the key wealth generating sectors of agriculture, energy and mining, whilst preserving and enhancing the ecology of freshwaters within the natural environment. Integrated water resource management (IWRM) was enshrined in the Act and it was the objective of the project to assist the new Catchment Management Agencies in establishing their Catchment Management Plans, through a process of technical evaluation and stakeholder participation.

My role was to advise on all aspects of water conservation and demand management, with the municipal sector being given special priority in line with the government's aspiration to achieve a minimum level of service to 'township' communities, many of which lacked continuity of supply. Often there was sufficient water at source, but high levels of losses, both 'apparent' and 'real' (also known as 'administrative and 'technical' losses), resulted in shortages at the consumer's tap. Thabo Mbeki had replaced Nelson Mandela as the county's president, but the latter's rainbow nation idealism and optimism about a better future for disadvantaged groups in society was still prevalent. Policies such as 'free basic water', aimed at improving the quality of life of the country's poorest citizens, had been introduced.

From Denmark and the UK we fielded a resident project manager and various visiting specialists. The project manager had his own house, but other members of the expatriate team were accommodated predominantly in the Battiss Guest House, an attractive property in the Pretoria suburb of Menlo Park. Designed in 1939 by architect Norman Eaton for world-famous South African artist Walter Battiss, it had eventually passed to Ray Zeederberg who ran it as a guest house, whilst respecting and preserving its original and unique character.

The fine properties in that leafy suburb, and others like it, were fitted out with security fencing, gates, CCTV cameras and notices prominently displayed around the boundaries declaring that this or that security company was employed and if called out there would be an armed response. This was standard practice in the cities, but less so in smaller rural towns, such as at Clanwilliam in the Western Cape where we had one of our pilot water conservation projects. For additional personal protection Ray had two dogs, pure bred standard poodles, Carol, the mother, and Toby, the son. Toby was a larger than average example of the breed and had the capability of exhibiting a level of aggression that could be just as off putting to a potential intruder as a Doberman or a German Shepherd.

As a late-middle-aged white male from the former colonial power and with no prior experience in that country, I approached my first meeting with my counterparts in DWAF, Michael Singh and Nigel Adams, with a degree of apprehension. Might I have an ingrained and/or unconscious bias or attitude problem that would be a barrier to the kind of mutual working relationship that was needed in the post apartheid era? I sensed their reservations and as best I could I explained about the kind of partnership projects that I had been working on. I tried to move the conversation on to key technical issues about which they had concerns and give the impression that I was ready to roll my sleeves up and get on with the job.

It was a good many months later, after some heavy going stakeholder workshop sessions, and equally heavy partying at a brai afterwards, as the music and dancing with all races and ages 'putting themselves about a bit' was in full swing, that I felt that I had gained a degree of acceptance and trust. In 2001 Michael kindly agreed to be my co-author of a paper on "Financial Considerations in Integrated Water Resource Planning for Local Authorities" delivered at the annual conference of the Institute of Municipal Engineering of South Africa (MESA).

The project model was for Carl Bro to be a managing consultant, overseeing and coordinating the work of local service providers, who did much of the groundwork and had to build relationships with the relevant stakeholders. The selection and appointment of service providers meant applying positive discrimination protocols that were designed to give opportunities for young and emerging firms and groups, especially those employing historically disadvantaged individuals. Contracts for packages of work were awarded on the basis of a combination of technical merit, team members and price, using a points scoring system. In the diversity column, since women were seen as having been at a disadvantage too during apartheid, the highest points were awarded for a black woman, whereas at the other end of the spectrum, the least was given for a white male, like me(!).

A few years later I was reminded of these means of introducing diversity criteria to an appointment process. The Chartered Institution of Water and Environmental Management (CIWEM), of which I was a Fellow, wished to appoint some new trustees. With motivation that I understood and respected fully, it expressed the wish to have a broader spectrum of trustees that was more representative of society as a whole, declaring that applicants from backgrounds that were presently under represented would be looked upon with favour and encouraged to apply. I obtained details of the application procedure, not intending to apply myself, but being interested to compare it with a process that did seem to work. I was disappointed as it seemed to me to be flawed, exhibiting a lack of transparency and rigour in the methodology, but my representations fell on deaf ears.

Offers came in both from well established firms and new entrants. The former were traditionally the domain of white males, so the procurement policy pushed them to recruit from a wider racial and gender pool. But that all took time and meanwhile there was still the need to deliver outcomes, so invariably such teams would be underpinned by engineers and technicians whose experience derived from working under the previous political and social regime. In my sector of the project we ended up with a reasonably satisfactory mix of long established consultants and emerging firms. In the latter category was the partnership of Toriso Tlou and Petrus Matji, exactly the kind of provider that the policy was designed to encourage.

Despite delivering success on our project, Toriso and Petrus then went their separate ways afterwards, but in a reversal of roles I continued to work on water conservation initiatives in a number of towns and cities, including Cape Town, as a sub consultant to Petrus's new company. He also employed me on the evaluation and upgrading of wastewater treatment plants, to assist him in becoming established in that sector. All went well with our relationship until a key municipal client of his ran out of money and stopped the flow of payments. I was left with a debt which I could live with, but for Petrus it was a bigger problem and he shut his company down when tempted by the offer of a well paid post within DWAF. Given the totality of my earnings in South Africa and the personal satisfaction that I had gained from it, I had no hard feelings on the matter and accepted the loss as part and parcel of the business of freelance sole trading.

I treasure an email that, on the conclusion of the DWAF IWRM project, was sent by Obie, one of the young and enthusiastic technicians who we engaged. It was addressed to CBI who forwarded it to me:

> September 9th 2004, from obzo@yahoo.com
>
> *"Dear Carl Bro, my name is Obie.*
>
> *How I love Carl Bro, I was a technician for the DWAF/DANCED Integrated Water Resource Management Project at Clanwilliam.*
>
> *Believe me it was a job completed well and I'm still happy about it.*
>
> *Please send my regards and greeting to a man called Hue Allan, it was a pleasure working with him and may the Lord bless him mightily.*
>
> *If there is any job here in SA that you are going to run I would be happy that you notice me by email."*
>
> *Thanks"*

Northumbrian Lyonnaise

Taking an active part in a professional body such as the ICE and in my case also CIWEM, attending meetings and being on committees, provides opportunities for networking. I had been a member of CIWEM and two of its predecessor bodies (the Institutions of Water Engineers and Scientists and Public Health Engineers) and had served on its local committee as Honorary Treasurer. Keith Eddleston was a colleague of mine on that committee and was employed by Northumbrian Water in their research centre, at that time owned by the large French water enterprise, Lyonnaise des Eaux, which operated in many countries across the world.

Keith was interested to learn what we had been doing under the SPRINT programme, and subsequently in Ireland and South Africa. I regarded it as an endorsement of our holistic approach to water conservation and demand management when he appointed us to assist them with drafting parts of Lyonnaise's Best Practice Guide on Underground Asset Management.

11 The UK Scene in the 1980 and 90s

Although now firmly embedded within Haiste's international department, and a change of company name to Haiste International Ltd. reflected our global aspirations, I still had opportunities to work on projects in the UK. I was keen to take them as I had seen engineers struggling to get back into the domestic mainstream after returning from long spells overseas. Extensive past international experience was not always highly regarded by prospective employers, as design and construction practices could be different and it was often felt that an engineer who had spent several years working overseas was likely to be out of touch with the latest practice in the home market.

During that period I was involved with a mixed bag of projects that included water and wastewater treatment plants, pumping stations and pipelines, and drainage area studies that addressed the structural, hydraulic and environmental deficiencies that are typically found in many of the UK's ageing urban sewerage networks.

For a time I was the firm's Supervising Civil Engineer, overseeing the training of graduate engineers under the ICE's structured scheme. This brought with it the job of recruiting new graduates for the Leeds office and I surprised a few old hands when I appointed the first female graduates. As far as I was aware there was never any gender issue within our office, the girls had no doubt been though some of that at university and could give as good as they got, if necessary. However one of our graduates complained to me that she was picked on by a superior on a construction site, during a secondment which I had arranged under a graduate exchange agreement that we had with a contractor. The matter was resolved in conjunction with my opposite number at the contractor, but it showed that in the 1980-90s our industry still had some way to go in the area of gender equality.

I had a similar role with technicians and at that time there were government schemes to encourage employers to take on school leavers – Youth Training scheme (YTS) and Youth Opportunities Programme (YOP). As these were both introduced by a Conservative government, naturally they came under attack from the opposition party, who portrayed them as just being a means of enabling exploitative employers to pay less than the going rate and with no guarantee of proper training. My experience is limited solely to the company that I worked for. All of our youngsters attended technical college under the BTEC scheme and went on to have good careers with us and with competitor firms when they moved on. Many turned out at a company reunion that I organised in 2010, a chance to reminisce about the good times that they had with us during their formative years.

A far-sighted decision that was taken by the Haiste management, one that proved to be fundamental to the firm's survival, was to embrace the opportunity presented in 1981 by the launch of the IBM PC. Two young PhDs were recruited, Roger Pyle and John Suter. They were to help establish the firm as one of the leaders in the fields of computer aided analysis of water and sewerage networks, the instrumentation and automation of water and wastewater treatment plants, and telemetry systems. As a computing novice I could never be in the front line of that business, but I sought to understand what was possible and thus in a project management role be able to bring that expertise to bear on infrastructure issues with which I was more familiar.

Other attempts at diversification and developing new areas of business came about as part of what to some extent was a bit of a reverse take-over. Anglian Water was a major client of ours and our directors had good relationships with its hierarchy. During one of Haiste's periodic bouts of corporate restructuring, Geoff Bowyer, who had recently retired from the board of Anglian Water, was appointed as our new chief executive. He brought in another ex-Anglian executive, Ian Ramsden, an energetic man brimming with self confidence, full of ideas and a single mindedness, not to say ruthlessness, when it came to carrying them through. He was known to us all as 'Rambo'.

I had crossed swords with Ian a few years previously, when I was Haiste's project manager on a sewerage contract at Sleaford in Linconshire. I was faced with having to address one of the industry's common sources of dispute between Engineer and Contractor, namely what constituted rock and the triggering of additional payment when it was encountered. I had tended to be broadly sympathetic to the contractor's basic position, but that was not how Ian saw it and I came under considerable pressure, not just from him but also from my director who was distinctly uneasy about having one of our best clients at odds with us. The contractor wielded his big guns, but he too was conscious of the need not to cut off a stream of future work from the same client, and so some kind of compromise settlement was arrived at.

The restructuring created a big company expansion minded model in which there was a group company, Haiste Group Ltd., with a small main board. Under that were several operating companies based on civil, structural and mechanical and electrical engineering, and automation, the latter breaking out beyond the boundaries of engineering infrastructure and into such areas as vehicle tracking and digital key systems. Ian carved out a piece of this pie by heading up a management consultancy and recruitment company, however Haiste Services Ltd. didn't survive after we were acquired by our new Danish owners, Carl Bro.

Leeds offices

When I joined Haiste in 1971 we were in Belmont House in Headingley. It comprised an Edwardian mansion together with its stable block, adapted as far as practicable to office use. A single storey extension was added to create a large open plan design / drawing office, but as staff numbers increased it proved necessary to establish an overspill office, which initially was within the British Steel office block in Kirkstall Road about a mile away. Later the overspill office moved closer to Belmont House above a shop in Otley Road, but this fragmentation was not ideal.

The directors cast around for larger premises and eventually settled on another old house conversion, or rather two adjacent houses that had been joined together. Together with an annex around the back, there was sufficient floor area for all of the departments to be accommodated on the same site. The architect who devised the conversion had been presented with quite a challenge in reconciling several different floor levels, the result was a distinctly disabled person unfriendly suite of offices with many sets of steps in addition to the main staircases between floors, as well as insufficient toilet accommodation!

Newton House was on the northern border of the Chapeltown district, which at that time had a somewhat unsavoury reputation. The nearest public house, The Hayfield, was raided regularly by the police in pursuance of drug dealers and the criminal fraternity generally. Eventually it closed when the council refused to renew its liquor licence; the building was later demolished. The new offices were however close to the border, although not within, the 'village' suburb of Chapel Allerton which is now one of the city's property hot spots for the trendy set.

When the announcement was made to staff, the directors declared that it was located in Potternewton, a sub district of sorts and technically true, but it didn't fool the employees and there were mutterings of discontent, rumblings about the safety of female staff after dark etc. The move was made however and in the 15 years or so that we were there, I do not recall any instances of violence against an employee. There were a couple of attempted burglaries and the odd theft from the car park, but no more than one might expect in other city areas.

At best Newton House was functional, just, but with the approach of the millennium it was becoming tired and compared poorly to competitors who were in purpose-built modern offices. Some of these were in new developments to the south of the city centre which, ironically, came under the jurisdiction of one of our clients, the urban renewal agency, Leeds Development Corporation. Carl Bro decided that it had to present both a better image to clients and be able to attract and retain high quality employees.

A final move took us a short distance to Grove House, which had been converted from a former nurses' home adjacent to Chapel Allerton Hospital and was on a shared site with new housing. I had my own office at Newton House, but as the move was coinciding with my resignation as a director of Carl Bro International (UK), I asked just to be allocated a desk in one of the open plan offices, for my use in the transition period to self employment. With the burden of company management lifted, I quite enjoyed being back in a general office, on an equal basis as it were to those around me and not being perceived as one of the bosses.

Scotland

Haiste had several branch offices in England and Wales but not in Scotland. An opportunity arose when a small mechanical and electrical (M&E) consultancy was being run down by its sole principal and owner, Jimmy Byers, who planned to retire. Strain and Roberston occupied a small office in the centre of Glasgow, had just two or three long standing jobs on its books that were coming to an end and nothing else in the pipeline. Being an M&E consultancy, it was logical for our M&E director, Derek Williams, to take on the job of running the office and to seek out new commissions, in the first instance just to keep the small number of existing employees in work. Derek had Scottish origins and had lived in Glasgow for a period of time. The objective was to grow it into a multi-disciplinary office on the basis of our track record in water and wastewater engineering, thus about 6 months after the acquisition I agreed to take over from Derek and try my hand at what for the most part was cold calling, not something that I was ever very good at.

I thought I would ease my way in by introducing myself to the two main existing clients, one of which should have been a potential source of new work for us. That client was Strathclyde Regional Council's Main Drainage Department, which serviced the wastewater needs of about half of the population of Scotland. Strain and Robertson had been their mechanical and electrical consultant for major works recently completed at Glasgow's largest wastewater treatment plant, Shieldhall.

The director received me in his office and it quickly became apparent that he wasn't a huge fan of consulting engineers, especially those from outside his patch, which is how he now saw Strain and Robertson since our taking it over (re-badged as Haiste Strain & Robertson). Having given him the usual spiel about our skills and experience, hoping that it might soften his attitude, I was taken aback when he revealed to me that his main reason for appointing Strain and Robertson was its *lack* of experience in wastewater treatment.

Basically what he had wanted, and had got, was a small team of broadly knowledgeable engineers who would do his bidding by drawing up unique specifications that were fully detailed in line with Strathclyde's requirements. The procedure had been to visit other large treatment plants on fact-finding missions and to encapsulate what was considered to be best practice in a 'pick and mix' bespoke specification. An off-the-shelf design for pieces of standard equipment would not pass muster and, whilst I understood his rationale, it must surely have come at a cost premium, borne ultimately by the Council's residents and businesses.

An immediate problem that I had to face was the approaching expiry of the lease on our city centre office and which the landlord did not want to renew. As well as looking for work, I was also checking out various offices that came within our modest budget. I wanted to be out of the city centre so as to have at least on street parking, but also a location that would give a reasonably good impression to clients. It brought me back to the Woodside area near Charing Cross, where Crouch and Hogg and other consultants and architects clustered. I was fortunate to find a suitable office that we could move in to, just in the nick of time before we were evicted from the old premises.

Coming on top of trips overseas, I was wearying of the weekly commute from Leeds to Glasgow. I did not wish to make my position there permanent, so I pushed the directors to recruit a full time and local replacement. When Ken MacDougall was appointed to that post I was relieved and looked forward to assisting him in the transition. However this coincided with Haiste's take over by Carl Bro, and the dust from that had still not settled when, still in acquisitive mode, the Danes then bought out a medium sized Scottish consulting firm, Kirkpatrick and Partners.

Kirkpatrick was active mainly in highways and building structures, so on the face of it they were a good fit with us, but it was a turbulent marriage and our small Scottish operation was caught in the crossfire in the battle for supremacy between the former Haiste and Kirkpatrick directors within Carl Bro UK. I was glad I was out of it and I sympathised with Ken who found that, unbeknown to us both at the time of his interview, he had taken on a bit of a poisoned chalice.

Pension fund

As a business in the 1970s, Haiste survived by expanding massively its international activities. A transition from the traditional partnership to a limited liability company, with directors in place of partners, facilitated injections of external investment that kept the show on the road in the 1980s. Again ahead of many of our competitors, the financial director, David Keegan, convinced the board to change the staff pension scheme from 'defined benefit', under which one received a pension of one sixtieth of final salary for each year of service, to 'money purchase' in which the company and the employee paid into an investment fund. With the latter model, ordinarily on retirement one would then purchase an annuity, with the option of taking part of it as a tax free lump sum. Self invested personal pensions (SIPPs) and drawdown plans that we are familiar with now weren't an option when the first money purchase schemes were launched.

The employees responded to the proposal with some scepticism, but the transition was made. An advantage not appreciated by employees at the time, was the removal of the dependency of the pension fund on the financial health of the company. When it came my turn to go into retirement I was grateful that I was in control of my own pension pot. I didn't have to face the prospect of being in a scheme like that of our erstwhile collaborator, Halcrow, hit by a toxic combination of company under-funding and central bank interest rate policy, having to be rescued in a restructuring that meant a diminution of benefits. It is a worry that one would prefer not to have in the run up to retirement.

Lagoon Technology International

It was common practice for UK consulting engineers to engage leading industry figures as external consultants. Typically they could be early retirees from the public sector, or academics who held positions of standing, encouraged to be involved with the industrial and commercial sphere, benefitting both the relevance of their research activities and the content of lectures to their students. Such consultants would often be paid a basic retainer fee in return for a degree of exclusivity with the firm.

Duncan Mara was a leading world figure in stabilisation pond systems for wastewater treatment, so when I learned that he had accepted a position as Professor of Civil Engineering at the University of Leeds, I persuaded the Haiste directors to explore the possibility of appointing him as one of our small group of specialist consultants. This was not an easy sell, not so much to the Haiste directors who were quite keen, but to Duncan, who had scant respect for traditional consulting engineers, like us, who he saw as promoters of ill-advised first world solutions in third world countries. He was justified in his view. Much international aid and loan funding was not well spent on sewerage systems and treatment plants, that were both inappropriate to the nature of the urban developments that they were intended to serve, and were expensive to operate and maintain, falling into a poor state of repair within a few years.

Fortunately for us, since we were not active in the mainly African countries where he was generally advising, we were able to start with a clean sheet with Duncan and were willing to buy into his appropriate technology mantra. We naively envisaged a relationship along similar lines to our other consultants, but that was not how he saw it. He was not going to confer his international reputation upon us and with modest input put his stamp of approval on schemes that we would design. He had a grander plan and he saw Haiste as the means of realising it.

Thus with his regular collaborator as a partner in the endeavour, Howard Pearson, a senior lecturer in microbiology at Liverpool University, and Haiste the third partner and provider of office accommodation and admin support as well as engineering expertise, a new company was born – Lagoon Technology International Ltd. (LTI). LTI recruited two full time engineering scientists, Steve Mills and Graham Alabaster.

As the originator of the Mara link I was keen to be involved in the LTI projects and I did manage to have some modest participation, especially when there was overlap with the conventional technologies with which I was familiar. The working relationship with Duncan and Howard was good and I came to realise, if I hadn't before, that the appendicitis that struck me in my final year at university, the timing of which pushed me into employment as a working engineer rather than going into academia, did me a favour. I was within my comfort zone as a project engineer and project manager but I recognised when I was in the presence of a person possessing an intellect that was on a higher plane than mine, such as Duncan – mastery of classical Greek was just one of his many attributes.

Understandably perhaps, our two academics were less at ease with the kind of financial discipline that we were used to at Haiste and which financial director David Keegan endeavoured to impose equally on LTI, both as a business and the profitability or otherwise of individual projects. LTI had a good run while it lasted, but it didn't survive the take-over of Haiste by Carl Bro.

12 Africa and Other Places

Tunisia

On the back of our experience in Baghdad and Athens, and with LTI being ideally placed to evaluate the city's existing Côtière Nord waste stabilisation pond treatment plant, in 1991 we were awarded a commission from Office National de l'Assainissement (ONAS) to prepare the Tunis Sewerage and Treatment Master Plan. Working with me from Carl Bro I was pleased to have Rosie Richmond, whose was equally at home with the hydraulic modelling of sewerage systems as she was with water distribution networks, and Dean Guesmia, who was originally from Tunisia's neighbouring country, Algeria.

Until relatively recently, when a fashion for corporate branding coupled with takeovers of many UK practices by American and European firms saw the departure of many names from the lexicon, British consulting engineering firms were invariably named after their founders, some being illustrious figures of their day. Haiste (John H), Halcrow (Sir William) and Howard Humphries, just a few of the long list that could fill a page in this book – Arup through to White Young (if there was a Z I have forgotten it!). French and Francophone consulting engineers generally leaned towards a different house style. Most that I came across were acronyms commencing with the letter S for Société (company) – in Iraq I had encountered SOGREAH and SAFEGE, and in Tunis our local partners were SERAH and SIRUS.

SERAH was our joint venture partner for the Tunis Master Plan project, but it was not an easy working relationship, brought about by a fall out between its principle, Mr Alouani, and his former number two, Mohnsen Tounsi. Tounsi had been named in our offer, but between bidding for the job and getting it, he had parted company with SERAH in less than friendly circumstances, to set up his own practice, SIRUS. Tounsi was well liked and respected by ONAS and Alouani had no alternative but to see the project through with Tounsi on board as a sub consultant, rather than as a SERAH employee.

Alouani could see that the Tunis project would be a launch pad for SIRUS as a competitor in the future, but instead of trying to keep us on side with a view to future collaborative ventures – after all we were not to blame for Tounsi's departure – he chose to be difficult whenever an opportunity presented itself. Consequently we were happy to see the back of him when the master plan project was concluded and we formed a new relationship with Tounsi's firm. Our first success together was a study of the sewerage and treatment plant facilities for the tourist island of Djerba and the development of designs for their augmentation.

It's in the nature of such projects overseas that one spends more time in the company of colleagues than is the case in the home office, usually staying in the same hotel, taking meals together and the odd touristic trip at the weekends. I accompanied a colleague when we flew out together on a trip to Tunisia, an affliction from which he suffered being known to me. He declined the offer of alcoholic refreshments from the drinks trolley and I thought that all was well. After a few days however, he called for a beer at dinner, I looked him in the eye and, with a practised reassurance that I imagine had been given to others on previous occasions, he declared that he was in control of the situation. I was hardly in a position to stop him.

The first beer was taken at a gentle pace and I left the dining room for a few minutes to take a telephone call. When I returned the waiter made a remark to me and I realised that we were now into territory that was familiar to my colleague but not to me. Somehow we got through the rest of the assignment and him on a 'plane back to UK.

Evening meals with Rosie were less fraught. I recalled the first time that I had been offered wine in our Baghdad hotel, in the pre-boom days when the choice of tipple was usually limited to beer, arak or whisky, or any combination thereof. Dining with Bernard Eagles, the waiter informed us that they had obtained some wine and would we like to try it, to which we gave a positive response, it was a first. The waiter knew the form, to pour a small amount into a glass for the customer to try. I did and it wasn't good.

"I'm sorry but it's corked" I said. He looked at me with some puzzlement. "Try it for yourself" I invited him, "sorry, but I'm a good Muslim and I don't drink alcohol". The wine in question was Algerian, which is the point of this diversion, and of course one would not condemn all wine from a region simply on the experience of one corked bottle.

Rosie and I decided that we would work our way through the hotel's modest list of local and foreign wines and compare notes, over a period of some days I might add and not in a single session. Eventually we came to a Cabernet, or perhaps it was a Pinotage, from Swartland in South Africa's Western Cape, it became our mutually agreed choice on all future occasions.

The master plan study duly concluded, we were asked to give a presentation to ONAS on our proposals for the largest of the city's existing wastewater treatment plants, Tunis South. I would have to lead it, but although most senior ONAS personnel had a fair command of English, indeed they were anxious to develop it so as to be able to participate in international conferences and the like and not be confined to networking in the Francophone world, I was persuaded by Dean and Tounsi to give my address in French. I was extremely nervous, but fortunately I had acquired most of the terms for all of the technical elements of a WWTP and I managed to stumble through it, in dreadful grammatical style, stalling at various points and looking to Dean or Tounsi for prompts. But my audience took it all in good part and when we moved into general discussion the atmosphere relaxed, to my great relief.

Morocco

We made efforts to obtain work in Morocco and with that aim I went as a delegate on a government trade mission, organised by the trade body British Water and led by the parliamentary Under Secretary of State at the Department of the Environment, Transport and the Regions, Angela Eagle MP. Dubbed by the press at the time as one of Tony Blair's 'babes', a label that I imagine she was not terribly keen on, she threw herself enthusiastically into what must have been a new experience for her. With an Under Secretary of State leading the mission, doors were opened at high level in Moroccan government departments.

A theme of such missions is to sell the message that UK practice is world leading and thus motivate the awarding of contracts to UK companies in the areas of interest. All of the delegates had a role in this endeavour and I found myself nominated to give a presentation on the treatment and re-use of wastewater sludge, a subject of which I had reasonable grasp of the basics but was far from being an expert. Fortunately I wasn't interrogated deeply on the subject, thus exposing the limits of my knowledge, and it drifted into a general discussion amongst those present.

With LTI we obtained a commission for the wastewater treatment plant at the town of Kenitra, which necessitated consideration both of conventional activated sludge and stabilisation pond systems, exactly the kind of project that we had in mind when establishing LTI. I spent many happy hours of mostly unpaid time devising an activated sludge plant design evaluation model within Excel. It stood me in good stead as I was able to develop it further on projects that came up in Europe a few years later.

Most of the Kenitra project details are a now a bit hazy, but what remains firmly embedded is a car journey there from Rabat. Our local partner in Morocco, Ahmed Chalabi, was driving. Tounsi from Tunisia was with us and occupied the front passenger seat, Dean and I were in the back seat of the Peugeot 405. It was dark, the traffic was heavy, and it seemed to me that he was hustling along and overtaking everything he came across at excessive speed. I was and am used to driving in what I will describe as a sporting manner, when road conditions permit and I am not carrying passengers, but this was unsafe and I asked Dean to get him to slow down, we were not late for an appointment so there was no need for it. I thought that would be enough to modify his style, but it had only limited effect and after a few kilometres it was as bad as ever.

He moved to pull out and overtake a truck, which turned out to be two trucks nose to tail. I saw the headlights of an oncoming vehicle coming towards us, but instead of braking and tucking back in behind, Chalabi put his foot down and seemed to be making for the gap between the lead and following truck, which was less than a car length. I braced myself for the impact, but before the tape of my past life kicked in he braked, swerved across to the left and mounted the roadside verge, avoiding the head on collision. We were on an embankment with a gentle side slope and we progressed down it. Fortunately it was planted with small bushes and not mature trees, the vegetation helped to arrest our progress and we ended up with the car on its side against one of the saplings.

Miraculously none of us was injured, just very badly shaken, we got out and it seemed the most obvious thing to do to see if we could dislodge the car from its resting place and get it back on the road. With this achieved, Chalabi continued to our destination, this time at a more modest pace and with not a word said. When we arrived I simply resolved that under no circumstances would I ever agree to be driven by him again.

Malawi and Mozambique

Carl Bro had a long established presence in East Africa, where there was a steady flow of Danish and international aid money. In 1995 the Copenhagen head office secured a commission to prepare a sanitation master plan for the city of Blantyre in Malawi, but they handed it over to us and I was appointed as project director. Another Brit, who had been on Carl Bro's books for many years, was appointed as the locally resident project manager. Mike Girling was familiar with the region and fortunately was used to undertaking projects in the manner proscribed by the African Development Bank, which was new to me.

Blantyre is Malawi's second city and commercial centre, a much larger conurbation than the small birthplace of explorer and missionary, David Livingston, from which it derives its name. The fact that city has retained its colonial name is indicative of the regard with which he is still held. I gained a few Brownie points with the city's administration by mentioning my schooling and early training in Hamilton, which is immediately adjacent to Blantyre in Lanarkshire and where the great man lived as an adult, during the times that he was not travelling around the African continent.

The transition from British colony of Nyasaland to independent state of Malawi had occurred a good many years before. Although the governing powers had changed, the lifestyle enjoyed by an expatriate in Mike Girling's position did not seem to me to be radically different to what it I imagined it would have been like in the colonial era. His wife, Jill, was an active member of the Women's Corona Society, an organisation that in 1937 had been established by the UK Government's Colonial Office to support wives of Colonial Officers, a wife's role then being understood to be that of looking after all of the domestic arrangements. The Society continues, but now in gender neutral form as Corona Worldwide[17].

Our project was just one of thousands that relied upon international agencies, such as the African Development Bank, to improve the lot of communities in third world countries. The process of going from identification of need to execution was formalised in a series of stages, the requirements for technical, economic and social appraisals being set out in comprehensive manner, leading to numerous reports and a timescale for implementation that could stretch out many years. Even once these feasibility studies, master plans and perhaps preliminary designs had been prepared and accepted by the donor agency and recipient government, it was still at the mercy of fluctuating budgets and priorities and it was not a given that a stream of money would follow immediately, if ever.

Our phase of the Blantyre sanitation project did however allow for the identification of minor works that could be implemented in advance of the main project, modest but worthwhile measures that could be carried out at low cost and without the need for importing costly equipment. Enter at this point our sewage works ideas man, Norman Cree, whose expertise and interest in 'making do and mending' had come about as manager of Dewsbury sewage treatment works in West Yorkshire when it was under local authority control, in those days having to compete for council funds with every other municipally provided service.

A phrase sometimes heard before 1974 was "there are no votes in sewage", reflected in the inadequate budget allocations for sewage treatment during the municipal ownership era. Some sewage works managers adopted a passive approach, kept the plant going as best they could and if the council wouldn't allocate the monies requested, then the plant would simply underperform accordingly. For Norman, poor performance of his treatment plant was not acceptable and he would be on continuous look out for clever solutions and fixes. After a few years working for Yorkshire Water Authority, as the less cash-strapped successor to Dewsbury council, Norman retired from that organisation and deployed his innovative skills enthusiastically and to good effect for us, at Blantyre and other places.

I was assigned as liquid and solid waste specialist on a project for the town of Tete in Mozambique, situated in the north of the country on the Zambezi River and about 200km by road to the west of Blantyre. The preferred way in to Tete was to fly to Harare in Zimbabwe and then to proceed by road.

In the 1990s, Zimbabwe President Robert Mugabe had still to put into effect his policy of ridding the country of the white farmers, by deploying his squads of veterans from the war of independence. The infamous Gideon Gono, Governor of the Central Bank of Zimbabwe, had not yet set his Zim dollar printing presses to warp speed economy trashing mode. Driving from Harare on a well surfaced road, the countryside beyond was either natural bush or well tended fields or pastures. Commercial activity in the towns seemed to be thriving and the school children were smartly turned out, boys in white shirts and grey short trousers, the girls in navy blue pinafore dresses of the style that was common in 1950s Britain.

Crossing the border into Mozambique presented a complete contrast. Only just recovering from a civil war, the roads were poor and the poverty of the people was evident in the ramshackle huts and ragged clothing. The land was generally uncultivated and if on the journey I felt the need to answer a call of nature, it would not have been wise to do so in a private spot off road, since land mines had been a common weapon of war and it would be years before it was safe to wander at liberty, a further constraint to recovery of the country's agricultural economy.

China

My only foray into the far east was a fact finding mission that I undertook for Carl Bro, who were bidding for a consultancy contract to upgrade the wastewater treatment plant for the city of Qingdao. It is a large port city of more than 6 million inhabitants on the western shore of the Yellow Sea, on the same latitude as South Korea to the east. In the colonial era it had been a German enclave, rather as Hong Kong was for the British and Macau was for the Portuguese. That had left its mark in both architecture and beverage. The old city, downtown Qingdao, could have been a transplant from Bavaria, with villas and public buildings built in an Alpine style. Tsingtao Brewery was established by the Germans and somehow survived

Mao's cultural and destructive revolution, its excellent product now being exported worldwide.

Typically on such fact-finding missions there is a briefing from the client at which all of the bidders are shown around the existing relevant facilities, in a group, jostling with the opposition. But on this trip I was able to visit the treatment plant with our local agent, unrestrained by the presence of representatives from rival firms.

After the site visit we were hosted in fine style in the client's executive dining room. The meal was served in a series of waves, with numerous dishes appearing. My experience of Chinese cuisine hitherto was limited to that nationality's restaurants as found in most cities and I barely recognised anything that I was presented with. Despite my not having previously encountered it deep fried on a plate, the features of a scorpion could be made out and I wondered at first if it might be a bit of chef's whimsy, constructed from some benign ingredients. It was crunchy and closer examination revealed that it did appear to be the genuine article. I managed to work my way through the first of the matching pair but concealed the second under a leaf of lettuce before my plate was taken away. I became aware that there was no rice in any form and I thought that rather odd. My local colleague explained to me that, in this part of China, rice was seen as an everyday peasant dish and not something that would be served to an honoured guest, which is what I seemed to be on that occasion.

Returning to Beijing I worked up my notes in our local agent's office and at the close of business he invited me out for a meal in a nearby restaurant. We were seated at a window table overlooking the street and had placed our food order, when two or three men arrived at the front door. Wielding sledge hammers, in a few seconds they reduced the door to a pile of glass fragments. Once inside they proceeded with similar violent intent on the large fish tank, but it resisted their attack as it was made from clear polycarbonate and not glass. The fish may have suffered from a form of shell shock, but afterwards they continued to swim around. Having failed in that endeavour the intruders turned to the cashier and removed bank notes from the till, then left the premises. It was all over in a couple of minutes.

Everyone including the cashier and waiters had been silenced and frozen to the spot, but then staff quickly came to the front door and cleared up the broken glass with dust pan and brush. I turned to my host to check on his reaction, which was not much more than a shrug of the shoulders. "I assume that they were behind with the protection money payments" he said. After about five more minutes the waiter appeared with our food and we continued as if nothing had happened. None of the other customers left the restaurant, the violence had been wielded on objects and not persons and at no point was any of the staff threatened – the cashier knew that it was wise not to put up any resistance.

13 Behind the Former Iron Curtain

The transition from employed operating company director to freelancer in 2001 went better than I had expected, leaving me wondering why I hadn't done it before. It meant the freedom to choose which assignments I would take, assuming that I was offered them, but losing the financial underpinning of a regular salary. Would I get my invoices paid in a reasonable time scale and without dispute as to the invoiced amount? How should I keep my books and did I need an accountant to handle tax and VAT? What insurance did I need – public liability, professional indemnity?

In my previous role I had engaged self-employed engineers and other specialists on behalf of my employers, so I knew the basics from the other side, gamekeeper turned poacher, and I was able to start off with reasonable confidence. Mixing with other freelance consultants I thought that some took a rather naive approach to professional indemnity insurance. Was I being over-cautious? I thought not as I had seen the big firms' insurers trying to pass risk onto external consultants through contracts of sub-consultancy as distinct from employment.

The Berlin wall came down in 1989, but it took some time afterwards for the political dust to settle and for the former Soviet satellite states in central Europe to establish political relationships with the European Economic Community (EEC), which preceded the European Union (EU). My move into freelancing self-employment took place when the European Commission (EC)'s programme of funding transport and environmental projects was in full swing, in what were known then as the accession states. In an arc from Estonia through to Hungary they were queuing up to join. EEC environmental directives had to be transposed into national law, after which grant aid became available for schemes that would improve the quality of drinking water, provide piped sewerage and treatment of waste in urban 'agglomerations' and reduce pollution. Bulgaria and Romania followed a few years later.

You too can be an economist

Until I was assigned to my first EC funded project, my knowledge of project economics was rather limited. I was familiar with 'capex', 'opex' and 'net present cost' but internal and external rates of return were novel and I came to understand how the many quotes that are disparaging of economists had their origins.

Our economic advisor for the Trenčín Right Bank Wastewater Treatment project in Slovakia, David Walker, worked his magic with the 'externalities' and allocated value to the benefits of cleaner river water downstream of our new treatment plant. Doing away with collection of septage by road tanker and the connection of properties onto main drainage came into it too. He had his own Excel spreadsheets to do the basic number crunching and was happy for me to take them and work up various 'what if' scenarios myself to save time in passing them to and fro between us. I was well and truly an Excel nerd by that stage.

I had acquired the basics of Logical Framework Analysis on the SPRINT project, which proved helpful too. The Trenčín project was launched successfully and received funding from Brussels, one of the first or perhaps the first to have done so in that country so under the then new "Instrument for Structural Policies for Pre-Accession" (ISPA).

Slovakia

Trenčín

In common with the other Soviet satellite states, infrastructure projects in Slovakia (then as Czechoslovakia) were given to state owned consulting bureaus and construction firms to develop and to implement. After 1989 these entities were split up and privatised, spawning a range of consulting firms on the western European model, such as Hydroprojekt and Hydroteam in the water sector. Our local partner for the Trenčín wastewater treatment plant was Stavfin a.s, a small design and project management office that was owned by local construction firm, Vod-Eko.

Hydroprojekt was appointed to undertake the detailed designs, on behalf of the construction contractor, Doprastav a.s, which was another former state enterprise.

At our first meeting, Monika Čižnárová from Stavfin and I were mutually apprehensive. It was my first time in her country and I was new to this type of EC assignment; it was her first dealings with the EC bureaucracy and she faced a Brit that in our contract was named as the project manager and so-called "expert". (Although in EC speak virtually the whole team were experts of one kind or another, so the term didn't have quite the cachet that might ordinarily be associated with it in other spheres.) Fortunately over the following months we established a good working relationship, helped by the fact that my Slovak deputy, Peter Koreň, was known to and well respected by her.

It was a first for Doprastav too, in undertaking a contract using the FIDIC Conditions of Contract – at Trenčín, FIDIC's so called 'yellow book' for plant design and construction. Instead of employing their own expert in contract administration, one with the necessary familiarity with the FIDIC Conditions, Doprastav seemed happy to learn from me on the job. As well as their willingness to adopt the technical and financial administrative procedures which I proposed within the framework of a quality plan, I found myself in the rather unusual position of helping a contractor to present claims for additional payment. It simplified things a lot!

As the appointed FIDIC Engineer, more typically one would expect to receive a steady stream of claims, some justified others not, but all having to be processed formally according to the provisions of the Contract. Instead we had a fast track procedure in which Doprastav would come to me if they had a financial problem and I would offer my opinion on whether there was any basis for seeking additional payment; and if there was what they needed to present for it to be considered. Spurious claims that would simply have wasted everyone's time were stillborn.

I didn't see that as being in breach of my obligation to uphold the interest of the Employer, which I fulfilled when formally evaluating and administering those of the Contractor's claims that did have some merit. The government ministry department responsible for overseeing the project and for liaison with the EC was also on a learning curve, and what was essentially a non confrontational approach delivered a financial outcome with which both parties to the Contract were satisfied and which passed through the EC's audit procedures in a routine manner.

Nitra

As the Trenčín project was winding down, I was appointed as FIDIC Engineer on another wastewater treatment plant, for the town of Nitra. The contractor was a consortium of Slovak civil engineering contractor, Váhostav-SK a.s., and Czech process plant contractor, Královopolská RIA, both experienced and competent firms in their respective fields. They delivered a well functioning treatment plant to the municipality on completion, but in contrast to my experience at Trenčín, working relationships amongst the participants were less harmonious.

At Nitra the contract was let on FIDIC 'red book' Conditions, under which a Contractor simply executes the designs that are presented to him. As far as the civil works are concerned, the contractor should be provided with designs and drawings that are fully detailed and able to be used on site for construction without much more by way of elaboration. But neither the municipality, nor the central government agency responsible for project oversight and channelling of funds from the EC, had appreciated a fundamental feature of a contract of this nature, namely that designs which are prepared for tendering purposes before contract award will inevitably be subject to change after the mechanical and electrical process equipment is procured. The civil works must be made to accommodate the plant, not the other way around. There was no provision either in the works contract or in our supervision contract to make these revisions, which turned out to be quite substantial, exacerbated by shortfalls in the details of the original tender designs.

I pushed hard for the firm responsible for preparing the tender designs to be appointed to undertake the necessary revisions and supplementary designs, but encountered considerable resistance. The client took the view that the designer had already been paid once for preparing a set of detailed designs that should be fit for use on site and they were unwilling to pay him a second time to revise them. The designer of course claimed that he had fulfilled the terms of his original contract – the designs had been signed off and he had been paid, job done and anything else should be the subject of a new commission.

My deputy, Pavel Klein, went some way to ameliorating the situation by producing some supplementary details, but it could not be a substitute for what was really needed. A further complication was the necessity for formal certification of the constructed designs under Slovak construction regulations. Pavel was on the register of engineers authorised to certify designs, by personally signing and rubber stamping designs and drawings, but he could not take responsibility for certifying the design of a whole element, as his input constituted only a part, nor was that onus upon our firm contractually.

It was an impasse that took months to resolve, but meanwhile work was underway on site and the contractor was soon submitting claims for delay and disruption caused by omissions in the designs provided to him. Eventually the ministry and municipality relented and a supplementary commission was awarded to the original designer, but it was limited in scope as its terms reflected to some extent their original stance on the matter. It was a continuing battle to have all of the designs concluded. The final cost of the delays and disruption was well in excess of that of a design support services contract, if one had been in place at the start of the job.

My relationship with Nitra's project manager was strained. I often found myself at loggerheads with him when I had to certify interim payments to the contractor. It was a fundamental difference in approach, his coming from practice that Pavel explained to me had prevailed in the Communist era. It was not helped by an unnecessarily complex payment certification format, which the government ministry department responsible had imposed as a budget monitoring and control tool. It could work for a 'yellow book' contract but for 'red book' it was inherently flawed. Further misunderstandings arose in the use of provisional sums, variation orders and contingency expenditure. My representations to the ministry didn't go unheeded however, as at a workshop which they organised on the financial management of ISPA projects I was given an opportunity to try to get my message across.

I was distinctly under the weather during one payment certification meeting with the project manager and my deputy. As it dragged on in its predictable manner, I lost patience and erupted in an outpouring of intemperate language and desk banging. They were taken aback, I apologised immediately and our session wound up quickly afterwards in a subdued atmosphere. I returned to my apartment and lay on my bed for several hours in the traditional darkened room.

The next day I drove to Trenčín to attend a meeting there and when it was concluded Monika said "you're not well are you Hugh?" I didn't put up much resistance to her proposal that I should go with her to see a hospital doctor whom she knew. I felt a bit like a child being taken by his mother. He examined me and declared "I'll need a chest X-ray". Monika produced a card of some kind that I didn't recognise, but it didn't seem to be a means of payment which would have been down to me. I was wheeled into the radiology department where the X-ray was performed and after half an hour or so I was back with the doctor. The X-ray plate's sleeve had the patient's name – Monika Čižnárová! "You have bronchial pneumonia" he concluded, "I'll give you a prescription, go to bed for a few days, drink plenty of fluids and don't get on an aeroplane back home until you are sure you feel better". I did as he advised.

Towards the end, Nitra's original project manager with whom I had had many battles, left, to my relief. His replacement was tired of it all and just wanted to get the job wrapped up. A final account with the contractor was eventually settled, after the usual horse trading. All of the confrontation over the interim payments became of little relevance.

Nitra was the origin of one of those long odds coincidences that come up occasionally. I had two buy-to-let properties in Leeds at the time, one was a student property and it was being advertised for the next academic year. While in my office in Nitra I had an email enquiry from an Anna Kunova, who being an 'ova' I recognised as being of central/eastern European origin. I asked her where she was from, Slovakia was the reply, and to my follow up question she replied Nitra! She was amazed to learn that I was sitting at a desk just a couple of kilometres away. Later that day I met Anna at her local college and signed her up as one of my tenants.

Zemplin

Trenčín and Nitra are in the west of the country, close to its borders with the Czech Republic and Austria. It was apparent in the first decade of the twenty first century that recovery from the previous half century of unsuccessful economic policies was well under way. In Slovakia's most eastern province however, growth was taking place at a much slower pace. South East Zemplin is situated close to the country's eastern border and a sewerage and wastewater treatment project there was to be prepared for EC funding.

At the kick-off meeting with the Ministry of Environment in Bratislava we discussed the broad scope of the project and it was noted that there would be many kilometres of pipelines to be laid. "Don't imagine a heavily mechanised work site in that region" I was told. "There is high unemployment and the project can provide jobs for manual labour. Unit costs for pipeline construction will be significantly less than you have experienced in the west, so be sure to check out local rates". The Ministry's project manager confided in me afterwards: "don't worry too much if the economic appraisals look a bit marginal, just be sure to make reference to Roma communities there and that will carry it over the line".

Prejudice against the Roma in Slovakia was something of which I was well aware. Invariably they were referenced in scathing and negative terms. The EC had social programmes running, designed to counteract stereotyping and to encourage integration. The main settlement in our area was Pavlovce nad Uhom and on our first day we were received by the mayor. He volunteered the information that there were many Romas living in the town, settled families not travellers. "We have a small sewage treatment plant serving a part of the town and if we go there we will pass through the Roma village. You may be surprised at what you see; if we stop I will be recognised and well received there as I have good relations with their community." It proved to be just as he said. The houses in the Roma village were built in rather more garish style compared with the architecture of the rest of the town and included some impressively sized villas.

The project went through without any great difficulty and after having completed the tender documents for procurement of the works my involvement came to an end. When I started out in this business I didn't imagine that it would take me mushroom picking in a forest that straddled the border with Ukraine, but an invitation from the mayor to join his small foraging party one weekend would have been churlish to refuse. Around an open fire afterwards and fortified with shots of slivovice, I convinced myself that my hosts had survived many such outings and were well able to distinguish between the edible and poisonous varieties.

Bulgaria and Romania

Projects that came up for funding had often been on the books for some considerable time, dating back to the previous political regime, but they lacked the finance for implementation. Getting a project accepted by the EC meant making a case for it in accordance with their guidelines. Out of a dozen or so projects that came my way I came across only one that I had doubts about.

Pazardjik

In the 1980s, construction had started on a water supply scheme for the town of Pazardjik in Bulgaria, but the money had run out and it was mothballed. The authorities wanted to reactivate the scheme and Carl Bro was awarded the commission to undertake the necessary technical, financial and economic evaluations to prepare it for implementation. After a fact-finding visit to the town and study of the scheme plans, it was apparent to me that it was just not viable and had negligible chance of standing up to EC scrutiny. It meant a loss of fee income both for me and my employer, but I advised that it should be stopped and no further money spent on it. It didn't make me popular with the Bulgarian authorities and I was summoned to Brussels to be interrogated on my report, but they were convinced and the plug was duly pulled.

Arad

> *"It's unwise to pay too much, but it's worse to pay too little. When you pay too much, you lose a little money – that's all. When you pay too little, you sometimes lose everything, because the thing you bought was*

> *incapable of doing the thing it was bought to do. The common law of business balance prohibits paying a little and getting a lot – it can't be done. If you deal with the lowest bidder, it is well to add something for the risk you run, and if you do that you will have enough to pay for something better."*
>
> John Ruskin, 1842

In Bulgaria and Romania I was appointed to a number of tender evaluation committees, both for construction works and consulting services contracts. The EC had gone to some trouble to try to eliminate bias, favouritism and downright corruption in the procurement process and to that end had devised a set of rigid procedures in their Practical Guide to Contract Procedures for EC External Actions (PRAG). Utilising these to draft tender documents which facilitated objective evaluation was a skill in itself, one that was not always mastered. Ambiguities were often found that bid evaluators had to wrestle with, but overall the guidelines themselves were soundly based, in my view.

Irish consultants, Project Management Ltd. (PM), recruited me as "Procurement Expert" for a €14m contract to upgrade and extend an existing wastewater treatment plant at Arad, a city in the west of Romania not far from the border with Hungary. It gave me an opportunity to develop my own ideas on setting out detailed procedures for administrative, technical and financial checks of tenders received. I developed a suite of standard forms that all members of the tender evaluation committee used to record the results of their scrutiny of the bids. The European Bank for Reconstruction and Development (EBRD) were providing about a quarter of the funding as a loan for the project and it had been determined that EBRD tendering procedures should apply. PRAG was utilised however to supplement the EBRD guidelines where appropriate.

The tender evaluation committee comprised several senior employees from the project's beneficiary, Regia Autonoma Apa-Canal (RAAC), myself and PM's resident engineer, Lester McIlwaine, an Ulsterman who lived in Arad with his American girlfriend, Kim, family dog and saxophone. Also in our team was Professor Anton Anton from Bucharest University, acting as external adviser. Like me he was interested in the workings of water distribution systems, but unlike me he had written a book about it and he duly presented me with a signed copy. It was in Romanian naturally enough, so I wasn't able to take too much from it, but I appreciated the gesture. An EU/EBRD observer attended many of the sessions.

Bids were evaluated financially on both capital and running costs and the cost difference between the two lowest bidders was extremely small. Shortcomings in the content of the second placed offer had resulted in a more extensive series of questions and answers between the evaluation committee and that bidder than with the others. The rules stipulated that such dialogue could comprise only clarification of the original offer and we took great care to ensure that the bidder didn't take advantage of this process to make adjustments to his original tender, to the disadvantage of the others. Arguably there were grounds for rejection, but we chose to give the benefit of the doubt and kept it in play.

We gave the second placed bidder every possible consideration, within the constraints of the evaluation rules, but when the result was announced he objected and embarked on a series of unwarranted criticisms of our evaluation. He alleged that we had not properly understood or evaluated his offer and went into some detail on matters where he believed, erroneously, that we had got it wrong. It was true that the content of his original offer and subsequent clarifications made our task more difficult than it should have been, but we stuck with it. When his criticisms fell on stony ground the bidder upped the ante by sending in a lawyer's letter, threatening all manner of dire consequences if we failed to take heed of his concerns. It was an attempt to harass and browbeat us into submission.

The evaluation had been conducted in closed session so what grounds did the bidder have for believing that we had not properly evaluated his offer? His response was that the questions that we put to him to clarify his offer had led him to this conclusion, but that was just not credible. Our questions were carefully phrased in a straightforward and 'closed' manner that did not reveal any opinion that we may have held, we simply needed him to provide information that was not present in his original documentation and to clarify where there appeared to be ambiguities. The bid had only just cleared a first pass hurdle where we had to decide whether or not a tender was "substantially responsive", i.e. errors and omissions were not of sufficient magnitude to bar the offer from further detailed evaluation. It was an example of our benefit of the doubt approach.

Despite all members of the tender evaluation committee having signed Declarations of Impartiality and Confidentiality, as stipulated in PRAG, perhaps we had a mole. But even if that was the case I never had a moment's doubt about the thoroughness with which we had gone about the task, or the robustness of its conclusion, which was signed off by all members of the committee.

Supported by the EC Delegation's office in Bucharest, where their technical adviser, David Noakes, was a former colleague of mine from Haiste and Carl Bro, we reported the bidder's objection to the EBRD. They scrutinised our evaluation and found no fault, our original report and recommendation was upheld. Time and effort by the various participants had been wasted in a fruitless endeavour that resulted in the project being delayed by several months, as we could not conclude a contract with the successful bidder until the procedure for dealing with objections had run its course.

Constanta

A friend of mine from Slovakia had been working for Finnish consultants, FCG-Plancenter, who found themselves in some difficulty with a works supervision contract that they had in Constanta, Romania's Black Sea port and tourist resort. He had given my name to FCG in connection with a design and construct works contract for treated effluent marine outfall pipelines serving the main city of Constanta and the nearby town of Eforie to the south.

I wasn't interested in taking on another new supervision contract that could easily last for three or four years, but FCG's silver-tongued director explained to me by that construction should be completed in another three or four months. Their supervisor and FIDIC Engineer was ill (I didn't ask and he didn't say), and they urgently needed a replacement to finish things off. Allowing for a 12 month defects notification period after the end of the construction stage, it should have meant an assignment lasting about 18 months. I signed a contract with FCG that had an original budget for six visits and a total of 50 days of input. I made my first visit to the project in October 2008 and finally concluded in the same month four years later, after seventeen visits and 138 days of input.

After my first day in the project office I was invited to dinner by our local manager and was surprised to learn that it would be an opportunity to meet my Finnish predecessor. His illness was of a similar nature to that suffered by my colleague in Morocco a few years before. He was married to a Romanian lady and was continuing to live there. He offered to help clarify matters that I was unable to glean from the files or from other project staff. I took advantage of his offer a few times until I got bedded in.

The contract was not in a good way. FCG was the second consultant, brought in after the first was dismissed, so the project had an unhappy history. There were several unresolved technical and contractual issues between the contractor and the municipally owned water and sewerage undertaking, SC Raja SA. Raja were themselves constrained by close oversight from the Ministry in Bucharest, in the form of the Central Finance and Contracts Unit (CFCU). That body was wedded to the 'hard-ball' philosophy of contract administration. I threw myself into these long-standing sources of conflict between Employer and Contractor and presented them with my findings as I saw them under the terms of the FIDIC Contract, not necessarily supportive of the RAJA and CFCU positions in all respects.

The works contract had become bogged down in delays arising from the contractor suspending work following failure either to certify payment that the contractor considered was due (the responsibility of the Engineer) or failure to pay the contractor the amount certified by the Engineer (the responsibility of the Employer). This was compounded by a series of claims for extensions of time with costs arising from what the Contractor considered were adverse weather conditions, and the Engineer's failure to issue formal determinations of these claims.

The Engineer (us) had been reluctant to determine the claims without first having obtained agreement with the Employer, but having failed to reach that agreement the matter had simply been allowed to drift. It was a mess. I spoke to the project director in Helsinki. Was he personally now going to take a more active role in fulfilling the responsibilities of Engineer that his firm had taken on, or did he want me to do it? If he decided on the latter course then since I wasn't a full time senior management employee of his firm, but a freelancer, I would need a Power of Attorney formally authorising me to act in that capacity on their behalf. I was pleasantly surprised that he issued it without any further ado. He was probably relieved that I was prepared to accept the responsibility. To my further surprise, Raja and the CFCU accepted it without question.

In the meantime, having lost patience, the Contractor had referred the matter to the Disputes Adjudication Board (DAB). The 'Board' in this case was a single individual, Gwyn Peredur Owen, MSc CEng FICE, FConsE FCIArb, an engineer with wide international experience and well versed in the adjudication of contract claims generally and the DAB procedure in particular.

None of the contracts with which I had been associated until then had ever reached such an impasse, so it was new territory for me. As FIDIC Engineer the claims that were now in the DAB's hands were out of mine, but the circumstances which gave rise to them remained in place and so further claims of a similar nature continued to be generated. Thirteen claims had been submitted to the DAB for adjudication and there was a further tranche that I was going to have to deal with as soon as the DAB gave his decision. The DAB procedure bought me sufficient time to examine the claims thoroughly, analysing the impacts on the programme of work due to stoppages, and scrutinising statistics on wave height and wind speed. I came to what I regarded as a robust basis for resolving the claims in my determination and was ready to go with it.

After a formal hearing in Bucharest, at which both sides put their cases and had legal representation, the DAB duly issued his decision. It disappointed both sides but the Contractor accepted it. In accordance with the terms of the Contract I issued a payment certificate for the amount due. Having sought legal advice CFCU refused to pay, on the grounds that it intended to challenge the DAB's decision. I didn't agree 100% with the DAB's decision either, but I was in no doubt that CFCU was in breach of contract by not making payment of the amount that had been determined by him. If, at a subsequent arbitration, the DAB's decision had been reversed in favour of the Employer, then the final payment to the Contractor would have been reduced accordingly. So yet again work on the project was suspended by the Contractor – more claims, more cost, yet more self-inflicted wounds.

If the reader wonders how it was that, as an engineer, I disputed the interpretation of a legal document made by a qualified lawyer, I came to my firm position on the basis of many years of experience dealing with those Conditions of Contract and their predecessors. Their origins date back several decades to Conditions which had been developed in the UK by the Institution of Civil Engineers and I had worked with them since I was a trainee. I had the added and unfair advantage over the Romanian lawyer that my mother tongue was English and I was in no doubt that the lawyer's interpretation of the relevant provisions was incorrect, as I saw it being skewed towards what her client wanted to hear.

By this time my employers were becoming edgy about the decisions that I had made and they feared for their continued engagement on the project. The CFCU had dismissed a previous consulting firm whose performance they had been dissatisfied with, so might they now have FCG in their sights? I thought at one point that I might be for the chop, but FCG's director and local manager both agreed to back me up. Eventually, after much anguish and brinkmanship, the CFCU and the Contractor agreed on a so-called 'Amicable Settlement', and both parties accepted my approach to and determination of the outstanding claims.

I had had to immerse myself in the contractual disputes, but out on site three large hydraulic systems were nearing completion and for me that was more interesting. It was akin to a full scale hydraulics experiment – when we commissioned the outfall pipelines, would they perform broadly in line with the original design calculations? I instructed the Contractor to produce a set of performance graphs for this purpose, to be included in the operating and maintenance manual as a baseline for longer term monitoring of pipeline condition, particularly detection of diffuser blockage.

It is common practice for a contractor to do a dummy run, to make sure that everything is in order before inviting the supervising engineer to come and formally witness it. In this instance it would have been apparent immediately that for one of the lines the results were badly out of sync with the design. Rather than coming clean about it, when submitting a second draft of the operating manual for my approval the opportunity was taken to substitute a graph which I had already approved, with a different one that was compatible with the field test. I was lucky that I spotted the sleight of hand. I dug out the original design calculations and uncovered an error that shouldn't have been made by an undergraduate student.

I presented my finding to Raja, expecting to be complimented on my diligence, but instead I and my predecessors were criticised for allowing it to arise. Potentially the consequences could be quite serious for all concerned we were informed. The contractor came up with various excuses in an attempt to defend the indefensible, but that didn't solve the problem. Having by now established where the defect lay, a simpler and less sophisticated design for the flawed hydraulic element emerged, but at least one that could be made to work. The contractor didn't put up any more resistance and, to my relief, the client accepted the corrective measure. In my fifty years of professional practice it was the one and only time, of which I was aware, that I encountered a deliberate act of deception in an attempt to cover up an error.

14 An Expert at Last

"An expert knows more and more about less and less and finally knows everything about nothing".

Attributed to Konrad Lorenz.

Despite having held several positions as an "expert" on EC projects, I didn't consider myself to be any more than a reasonably competent and diligent professional with sufficient breadth of experience gathered over the years to enable me to manage multi-disciplinary teams. In any of the subject matters that I dealt with I wouldn't have had too much difficulty identifying others in those fields with more right to be accorded that label.

Being an expert witness in civil litigation proceedings is a bit different however. In the subject matter of the case, the parties expect to benefit from a relatively high level of expertise from their expert, who, if he or she isn't on top of the subject, may get into difficulty as it proceeds. It happened to me on one occasion – a commission that I took on in the expectation of deploying my skills in matters of drainage, turned out to need expertise in carpet under-lays, a subject on which the expert appointed by the opposing party had more knowledge than I.

Expert witness work started to come my way around the time I was preparing to leave Carl Bro and embark on life as a freelancer. Significant numbers of experts that fish in that particular pool are sole traders rather than employees of professional practices. When I contemplated the composition of this memoir I thought that the cases that I had been involved in would provide a rich seam that I could mine for a chapter of interesting anecdotes, with intriguing sub-headings such as "the white goo", "the churchyard bones" and "ankle deep in the night club". But I realised that I was going to be constrained on the grounds of confidentiality.

I was engaged as an expert witness on about fifty cases, but of those only four got as far as a hearing before the judge in open court, at which point the matters in dispute entered the public domain. Three of those concluded within a couple of days of the start of the hearings, as a result of settlements being agreed at the eleventh hour, saving at least some of the cost of the court, barristers fees etc. The fourth collapsed on the first day because a witness was unable to convince the judge of his veracity, a key element of my technical analysis being reliant upon his reported observation (as I had made clear in my report).

All of the other cases either didn't proceed after I had submitted my report, which hopefully brought some technical clarity to the parties and their legal representatives concerned, and/or the case was settled out of court on terms which were confidential between the parties. Following settlement in a case of very substantial value, in which professional negligence had been alleged against a firm of consulting engineers, a household name in our business, the instructing solicitor informed me that, not only were the terms of the settlement confidential, but the fact that the proceedings had taken place at all was to be confidential and under no circumstances should I reveal that they took place.

Professional negligence

I had been engaged as an expert witness a couple of times before on relatively small matters, but I was really a novice in the business when Carl Bro were appointed in a case of high value, one of alleged professional negligence against an architect, following the discovery of significant defects in factory drainage and related works. Six experts participated, covering different specialisations, three on each side. With me was a colleague and quantity surveyor who had recently been on an RICS training course and he had a valuable set of notes on the dos and don'ts of being an expert witness. I admitted to the instructing solicitor that my experience as an expert witness was somewhat limited, but that didn't seem to bother him too much. "You focus on the technical matters, don't worry, I will guide you through the process" he said.

I learned a great deal under that solicitor's watchful tutelage and signed up to the UK Register of Expert Witnesses which provided numerous helpful guidance notes and a regular newsletter. Subsequently I was accepted as a member of The Academy of Experts (TAE), a learned society which strives to uphold standards in that sphere. With TAE membership I was able to secure professional indemnity insurance on favourable terms and obtain appointments in my own right.

The case against the architect had been brought by his client, who had tried to get the job done on the cheap by limiting the scope of the architect's services and project managing the work himself. In works of construction there are overlaps between the scope of services potentially provided by an architect or engineer and the drainage of buildings is one such example. The pipes in question were below ground and both the architect and his client had regarded them as part of the building works. In reality they were more properly part of the industrial production process.

The legal test for negligence is whether the professional made a decision which no "reasonably competent professional" (and not an "expert" in his field) would have made, the so called 'Bolam' test – *Bolam v Friern Hospital Management Committee,1957*. What a judge would have concluded we shall never know because the parties came to a settlement before the court room drama unfolded. But I regarded it as not insignificant that, having dispensed with the services of the original architect, the Claimant considered it prudent to engage a firm of consulting engineers to advise on the remedial works.

The revised scheme that the engineers developed was of a high standard, understandably they didn't want to leave anything to chance, but it raised the question of whether it incorporated an element of betterment that should not be laid at the door of the architect, even if he was found to be negligent. Much of my time was spent negotiating with the Claimant's expert to try to agree what constituted a 'basic scheme of remedial works', being of lesser scope than the actual works which were implemented at considerable cost.

The Claimant's expert was an employee of the consultants responsible for the works in question and I didn't envy his position. He was reluctant to admit that his firm had produced a more expensive scheme than strictly necessary to rectify the defective works, whilst at the same time he appreciated that his primary duty was to the Court and to give his independent professional opinion.

Duty to the Court

It is not universally understood that an expert witness's over-riding duty is to the Court and not to the party who pays for his or her services. It was something I had to point out from time to time, a message that wasn't always warmly received. I was engaged as the Single Joint Expert on a case, directed by the Court with the aim of keeping costs down on what was a claim of modest amount. I had been nominated by the Defence solicitor as I was known to them from previous cases and the Claimant's solicitor was happy to accept me.

I turned up at the incident house, to be met by a hostile Claimant who I could not convince of my independence. I needed to go inside and it was only with great reluctance that he let me in. "Would you mind flushing your upstairs loo while I watch the inspection chamber in the driveway?" I asked politely. "No, I'm not doing your job, you should have brought an assistant." "Well if I had, the cost of the assistant would go on my bill which you will be paying if you lose the case. Why not just flush the loo and get it over with, I can do everything else I need outside and without further assistance." His more reasonable wife then appeared and agreed to do the necessary.

Flooding

Litigation arises when something has gone badly wrong. In my field many cases concerned water in some form being in the wrong place and causing damage. A few of those concerned clean water from the public supply system, a greater number were concerned with flooding of wastewater and/or surface water. In terms of legal liability there is a considerable difference between these sources of unwanted water.

Under the provisions of Section 209 (1) of the Water Industries Act 1991, a water supply undertaking has a strict liability if there is an escape of water from its infrastructure. It is not necessary to prove that the supplier is negligent. The incidents that give rise to litigation are generally those where there is a question as to the source of the water and/or whether or not the escape was from apparatus owned by the utility company.

It's less straightforward with sewage or surface water flooding. A sewerage undertaker does not have full control over what its customers pass into the foul sewerage network and is not expected to provide surface water drainage infrastructure that can cope with extreme climatic events. Legislation and case law reflect this, but in a number of cases that came my way in the late 2000s, plaintiffs were not convinced that inundation of their properties were caused solely by record rainfall that had caused widespread regional flooding on the incident days.

The starting position for the Defence in those cases invariably was to be dismissive of the claims, pointing to media and Met Office statements that reported rainfall that could be expected only once in a hundred years or more. It is not easy to explain that, in some instances, what is happening in short periods within a prolonged rainfall event can be more relevant, and that this requires an analysis of the data (if available) in 5 or 15 minute intervals, to establish if there are any 'spikes' of high intensity short duration.

In one case the affected property was in a village that had been flooded when the river burst its banks and inundated the lower lying properties. The property in question was on slightly higher ground and the flood waters did not encroach from below, but entered the property from above, when a small drainage ditch overflowed. I was able to show that the ditch had sufficient hydraulic capacity to pass the flow generated by rainfall on the small sub-catchment that fed it, but on the day in question that capacity was considerably restricted by obstructions in two culverts downstream, the first under a highway, the second through the garden of a neighbouring property. Liability was therefore a matter of the actions and/or inactions of the riparian owners of the two culverts and the 'act of God' defence failed.

In another case, some former industrial wasteland had been transformed for the better into an attractive country park. Whilst considerable care had been taken over the landscaping, with planting and wetland areas to encourage biodiversity, unfortunately the overall drainage of the site had not received the same degree of attention and on two occasions flooding had spread beyond the site boundary and into the basement beer cellar of nearby licensed premises. Like the first case culverts came into it, only in this instance it wasn't just a matter of blockage but whether or not there was a culvert at all.

The Claimant in the case informed me that he knew of a long time local resident who had recollection, as a child, of crawling through a culvert, at a point where logically there should have been one, but despite my probing around I could find no sign of it. Whether or not the landscaping scheme had increased the run-off from the site was not agreed between the three experts involved (there were two Defendants), but we all did agree that the scheme of works should have made provision for a culvert at the point where the old villager could recall his childhood play.

A house demolished

This was also a flooding case, one in which a developer's designer had deemed his responsibility to be limited to the boundary of the small site of expensive properties, mainly comprising former farm buildings that were sympathetically converted into modern homes within what was effectively a gated community. Unfortunately the designer of the site drainage neglected to take account of rising ground behind the development site, run-off from which encroached into the garden and on several occasions flooded the lower ground floor of one of the houses. The error was compounded by a failure to assess properly the level to which the adjacent river could rise. Under those conditions some of the site's surface water drains did not function as the designer intended.

The owner of the house was a quantity surveyor and development project manager. He was well able to get to grips with the reasons for the flooding of his house and he pursued the matter with some vigour, through his solicitor initially, but in a further misfortune the firm of solicitors that he employed and who had appointed me went out of business and he then bravely took it on himself to pursue the builder. I had devised a remediation scheme that could have been made to work, but it was always going to be seen for what it was, a fix of what had been a defective design in the first place. In the owner's opinion, it would adversely affect the value of the property if he was to sell it.

The case was closed as far as I was concerned and I heard nothing more for a considerable time, until the owner contacted me to let me know that my report had been helpful to him in his proceedings against the builder and that I might be interested to learn that eventually he had decided to take drastic action. He demolished the wing of the house that was affected and rebuilt it to a higher floor level. He told me that, despite what it was costing him, his feeling was one of relief that the several years of anguish were now behind him and that the forever home that he and his wife had dreamed of could at last be realised.

Age wins out over youth

As I made the gradual transition into retirement, I was increasingly aware that, in certain fields, technological change in our industry was proceeding at a faster pace than I was able or indeed wished to keep up with. However I felt that I was on safe ground when I was dealing with engineering issues from first principles, which is often what is required in matters of litigation.

In a case in which the purchaser of a property was suing the vendor over a septic tank which came with the property, being somewhat 'long in the tooth' turned out to be an advantage over an opposing and younger expert, who had condemned the septic tank as being unfit for purpose and not compliant with Building Regulations or the relevant British Standard. My instructing solicitor acting for the vendors simply wanted to know whether it was or was not a septic tank, and more particularly was it consistent with the regulations and accepted practice in 1931, when it was originally built?

There were no relevant statutory requirements in 1931, which also pre-dated the first publication of a British Standard on septic tanks. However I recalled having a text book back in the 1970s which, even at that time, was rather old fashioned and becoming out of date. I no longer had a copy, but I found one for sale on eBay. Many of the illustrations were as I remembered them, drawn in an old-fashioned style and consistent with the book's origins, its first edition having been published in 1936. One of the illustrations was of a septic tank that was not dissimilar to the item in dispute.

In 1908 a Royal Commission produced its Report on Sewage Disposal and this seminal document became a key reference that remained applicable right up until 1974 when the Control of Pollution Act was added to our legislation. The 1908 report had included recommendations on septic tank design with which the disputed tank complied. I was thus able to give clear and unequivocal answers to the solicitor's key questions. My younger opposite number was not wrong in his appraisal, but sufficient memory retention of how things used to be did prove to be advantageous in that instance.

Two care homes

At the age of around 70 I found myself engaged as an expert witness on two cases which concerned flooding to old persons' care homes. I had only ever been in one care home before, where my ailing father had been looked after for a short period to give my stepmother some respite. I did not come away with any particular impression, either good or bad. On the first case I was engaged by the solicitor for the Defendant, a major water and wastewater utility company. The Claimant was the owner of the care home, on the outskirts of a seaside town. It had been flooded on several occasions.

I arranged to meet the Claimant's expert on site, an engineer who I knew from an earlier encounter and with whom I was on friendly terms. Mike was a younger man than I but he was accompanied by an older colleague in my age bracket, his specialist in the operation of sewerage systems. We entered the premises and the atmosphere was undoubtedly institutional, a strong odour of disinfectant and cleaning products laced with flowery perfume prevailed. The older man confided in me quietly and echoed my thoughts, "this is the kind of place I don't want to end up in, as I would be leaving in a wooden box".

At the second care home, pleasantly situated close to a river in a Pennines town that was prone to flash flooding, a colleague who was starting out in the expert witness business had asked me to give him a hand in a complex case. He was especially clued up on hydrological matters and from time to time I had engaged him to assist me in that area, so I was returning a favour by offering second opinions and advising him on the procedural aspects.

After inspecting the river and its surroundings and the various paths that the flood waters had taken, we went into the care home with its owner. It was in complete contrast to the first, there was a reception desk as in a small hotel, we walked through the comfortable residents' lounge and dining area; the occupants knew the owner and greeted him warmly, the chef could be seen busy in the kitchen behind the serving hatch, the lunch menu was inviting and it could have been a smart down town bistro. If I had to end up here, I thought, I shouldn't complain.

Meetings of experts

Under Part 35 of the Civil Procedure Rules in England and Wales, each party appoints an expert who prepares a report according to the brief that is given to the expert by the instructing solicitor. Typically the expert appointed by the Claimant gets in there first, as his or her report is used to draft the Particulars of Claim. The expert appointed by the Defendant's solicitor is then expected to find whatever deficiencies he or she can in the Claimant's expert report and then to produce his or her own report, which may come to some different conclusions or at least question some of the analyses and interpretations of facts that the Claimant's expert has presented.

The Court is not keen on having to decide which expert's view is the more believable, and naturally would have difficulty in so doing when it comes to technical matters. The method of resolving this is to instruct the experts to meet and to produce a joint report in which they are required to set out which matters they can agree upon and which they cannot, and in the latter category they must give reasons for their disagreement. This is intended to narrow the specific technical issues in dispute and aid the Court in questioning the experts in the witness box.

However friendly one might be in social discourse with the other side's expert, the meeting can be a tense affair. The Claimant's expert is generally at a disadvantage, as it is easier to pick holes in the work of someone else than it is to produce that work in the first instance, starting with a blank page.

Whilst the agenda for a meeting can be dictated by the instructing solicitors, the clients' legal representatives should not be engaged in the dialogue. As a meeting of experts is proceeding, the solicitors on both sides are biting their fingernails, worrying about what their expert is going to agree to that may be disadvantageous to their case. I am sure that I am not alone amongst the expert fraternity in having taken a bit of an ear-bashing from a solicitor who felt that I had conceded a point that he would rather I hadn't. On the other hand I was also congratulated a few times on having squeezed a concession out of the other side. I emphasise that these constituted purely technical give and take; the expert must not become embroiled in any form of negotiation.

It is often only when sitting across the table from a fellow professional, with a set of plans or calculations under scrutiny and engaged in meaningful dialogue, testing one another's analyses and theories of causation, that a full and clear picture emerges in its full complexity. Litigation proceedings are rarely clear cut, if they were they would be resolved before getting to the stage of expert reports.

I found myself at an advantage in a case that concerned a major construction failure overseas. The Claimant decided to pursue his claim against the UK firm in an English court, which may have said something about the Claimant's view of the courts in his own country. The proceedings were therefore held in the English language, notwithstanding that the contract between the parties was written in the language of the country where the incident occurred. Instructed by the Defendant's solicitor, I was required to 'meet' with the Claimant's expert. We were thousands of miles apart and so as to avoid the cost of travel and accommodation that would be incurred in us being in the same room, we endeavoured to do it on the telephone. I was a bit disappointed as I was quite looking forward to a trip to a country that I had never before visited.

It was apparent at the outset that I had to take the lead as I was familiar with the rules of engagement in the English courts. I explained to my opposite number about our having to produce a joint report and I offered to do the drafting, even though convention would have put the onus on him. I tried to assure him that, in drafting pieces of text that he wanted to include, I would try to compose it in clear English as if I was in his position. I also gave him the opportunity to comment on the format of the report, subject headings and the like. Despite difficulties with mutual understanding at various points, after a couple of hours of discussion we did reach a position that represented a conclusion of sorts and I said that it was best now if I composed a first draft to send to him and give us both time and space to reflect and prepare for the next 'meeting'.

I wondered at the time if our exchange was being recorded in the conference call that had been set up by my instructing solicitor, and if in bending over backwards to assist my opposite number in the performance of his duties in circumstances that were unfamiliar to him, I might be subject to censure, but nothing was said. After the second draft of the report we had concluded things to a sufficient extent that, I like to think, assisted the parties who then, sensibly, reached a settlement that avoided a full blown court hearing.

A final case

It had been dragging on for years. Problems with funding the litigation caused a number of long pauses in the proceedings and each time the complex case sprung back to life, sometimes after more than a year, it was a bit of a struggle to pick up from where I left off. I had already decided that I was going to retire and I was declining new cases that were offered to me. It wasn't my fault that a case which should have been concluded in, let us be generous and say three years, stretched out over seven. I could have declared that on a certain day I would be retiring and if the case was not resolved by then they would have to find another expert to take it over, but I was acutely aware that this would put the long suffering clients in a very difficult position as it would bump up the costs with which they were already struggling. So when it emerged that, finally, formal proceedings were in hand that would lead to a court hearing, I agreed to carry on.

I had had meetings with the barrister since quite early on to review the legal issues that would form the basis for the proceedings. The solicitor was generally bullish and latched on enthusiastically to points that favoured his clients, but on one occasion I felt obliged to write to him and correct some of his understandings. It was one thing to throw everything at it when going for the Defendant's jugular, but he wasn't doing his clients any favours by over-playing the likelihood of success.

The final months of the case is a time I would rather forget. I had been hospitalised some months before and although signed off I was on medication, I was keen to de-stress but the administration of the case was poor. Important documents which I had been given previously were, unbeknown to me, incomplete, due to a sloppy bit of filing by the clerk who had prepared the dossier. I discovered the shortfall in content only at the meeting of experts, where I was embarrassed, since as a consequence some of my analyses were flawed. I left that meeting knowing that there was a considerable amount of further work to do.

It was extremely helpful to have the missing documents, but it needed a far more rigorous analysis of the causation if I was going to be convincing in further scrutiny, especially now that I had sight of the Defence expert reports. The Court had agreed that I could produce a supplemental report, but in a very short time scale in the run up to a Christmas break. My family was less than impressed by my withdrawal from full participation in the preparations for the festivities ahead.

Immediately after the break the barrister called me to a meeting at which he was going to develop his strategy for the hearing. He went through things with great thoroughness and in so doing he uncovered a potential weakness in the case that should have been identified and addressed right at the outset. The solicitor was highly critical as he saw the possibility of the case falling at the final hurdle. Inwardly I felt that I should indeed have picked it up, but it was as much a legal as it was a technical point and I deemed it to be on the barrister's shoulders too. Furthermore, in neither of the two Defence expert reports, nor in the formal Defence to the Particulars of Claim, had the matter been highlighted, so I was not alone in not having spotted it. In the event the case collapsed for a different reason entirely.

I did have regrets when I was approached to take on new cases that looked rather interesting and into which I would have liked to get my teeth, but that final case experience was the clincher in turning them away. At 70 years plus, although I remained reasonably active both mentally and physically, grey cells were dying off. I never wanted to be in a position of providing advice that might have fallen short of the standards that I believed to have set myself, and felt that I had achieved, over the 50 years or so of professional practice as a civil engineer, from apprentice to expert witness.

Timeline

1960-1962 : Hamilton Town Council Burgh Surveyor's Department. *Apprentice Civil Engineer*

1962-1966 : Royal College of Science and Technology, Glasgow [now University of Strathclyde]. *Student*

1966-1971 : Crouch & Hogg[1], Consulting Engineers, Glasgow. *Graduate Engineer then Assistant Resident Engineer at Balmore Water Treatment Works*

1971-1988 : Haiste & Partners[2], Consulting Engineers, Leeds. *Senior Engineer progressing to Project Director (Haiste International Ltd)*

1988-2001: Carl Bro International Ltd, Consulting Engineers, Leeds. *Project Director*

2001-2012 : Self Employed, generally as Team Leader or Specialist on overseas projects, working for British, Danish, Irish, Finnish and Spanish firms.
In the UK, engaged as an Expert Witness in civil litigation proceedings.

---

1 Crouch & Hogg later merged with Waterman and Partners to become Crouch Hogg Waterman. In 1997 the firm was taken over by consulting engineers Halcrow (originally established as Sir William Halcrow and Partners). In 2011 Halcrow was itself taken over by US firm CH2M Hill, which in 2017 was absorbed into Jacobs (also US).

2 Originally established as John H Haiste and Partners, Haiste later became a limited liability company, firstly as Haiste International Ltd then as Haiste Group Ltd. In 1988 Haiste were bought out by Carl Bro of Denmark. In 2006 Carl Bro was in turn acquired by Dutch consultants, Grontmij, and in 2015 that firm was taken over by Sweco (Sweden).

A Short Haiste History

Inspired by some notes on the early days prepared by Harvey Roberts for one of his 'leaving do' talks and with contributions from Bob Adcock, Ian Aldred, Steve Day and David Dawson.

Note: This text was prepared by the author for the Haiste 90 Year Reunion Bash in April 2010, it has been included without edit, resulting in some duplication with the book's main text.

Origins

After military service in WWI, John Herbert Haiste (JHH) took up employment as a railway engineer and soon afterwards, in 1920, he established his own consulting office which engaged in water, sewerage, sea defence and river engineering works, ie much the same mix that represented core business for the firm over the next half century. His offices were in Barclays Bank Chambers, Trinity Street, Hull. In the 1930s, employees at the time who continued with the firm well into the post WWII era and who would be remembered by many attending the reunion included Raymond Horne, Ken Nicol and Gordon Petch.

During WWII, JHH moved his centre of operations to Leeds and opened offices in Queens Square (nos. 4, 8 and 22). After the war, new employees who joined and remained with the firm for many years included Harvey Roberts (as an articled pupil), Fred Firth, Irene Latus, Elsie Cordwell and Anne Baxendale. Donald Bean, who had been JHH's chauffeur, ran the print department.

John H Haiste and Partners – 1950s and 60s

In 1951, with the business growing, the firm became a partnership with JHH as senior, the other partners being a Mr Hutchinson, Josh Sharkie and the redoubtable Oliver Cyril Rowe (dubbed Charlie by the staff), OCR being responsible for an office which had been opened in Gloucester.

In the mid 1950s there were many changes. JHH retired and Charlie Rowe took over as senior partner. The Hull practice of Silcock and Simpson was absorbed into the practice and the Leeds office moved to Belmont House in Headingley. David Ellis, Arthur Pavey (Gloucester) and Gordon Petch became partners, along with E C M Reid from Silcock, known as 'Jock' due to his Scottish origins.

In 1957 a Peterborough office was opened, in Bridge Street, opposite the town hall. Josh Sharkie was the partner in charge with David Dawson, Harvey Roberts and George Smith being there from the start. Harvey remembers George being a keen athlete in those days – after his road run he would dry out his sweaty kit on the office heater, giving the office a certain 'fragrance'. When later George moved to Leeds, Bob Adcock recalls the office being regularly reminded of his presence when he practised his trumpet playing.

Eight Haisters who joined in the 1950s are attending the reunion. Other stalwarts of the firm from that time – Alan Collins, Ken Richardson and Peter Hogan are, like George, sadly no longer with us.

Saturday morning working was still practised, but in the Leeds office, lunchtime sessions in the Skyrack would follow, with the partners standing the drinks – quite a benefit to the impecunious junior staff as Steve Day recalls.

The 1950s and 60s were golden years for Haiste and other consulting engineers, as public water supply and sewerage services were extended to serve the substantial numbers of households that, prior to WWII, relied on local wells, dry toilets and septic tanks. Full ACE scale fees on long pipelines and standard designs of pumping stations and treatment plants were not quite a licence to print money, but you had to mess up pretty badly not to make a good profit.

Irene Latus became head of admin and accounts and she controlled expenditure with an increasingly strong iron grip – if a draughtsman needed a new pencil he had to show the stub of his old one to the keeper of the stationary cupboard, which was under admin's lock and key. This control was routinely circumvented by chopping pencils in two!

Further management changes occurred when Charlie Rowe retired in the late 1960s, with David Ellis taking over as senior partner, Bernard Eagles and Harvey Roberts becoming partners.

Charlie Rowe had a fiery temperament and would engage in rows in the office when things were not to his liking – Bob Adcock recalls that one of his sayings was "you've no more sense than a nit on a monkey's balls"! Steve Day remembers him annotating drawings with "balls" in large letters. Amongst the staff therefore, his departure was greeted with some relief. However he was once on the receiving end when, believing that Charlie was having an affair with his wife, the husband of the senior tracer physically assaulted him.

In 1966 a separate structural department was formed, initially under Ian Aldred – this was the first indicator of the partners' desire to expand the range of the firm's services. A few years later an M&E department was established under Ken Barker, with Alan Higgs as his no. 2, later joined by Arthur Burgess on the electrical side.

Haiste was often at the forefront in promoting new ideas – submersible pumps, screw pumps, aeration, biodiscs, novel sludge treatment systems etc. The partners had an entrepreneurial streak and embraced the concept of marketing well before most of their peers. Charlie Rowe's right hand man was Fred Firth, not a qualified engineer but a natural salesman with a photographic memory who brought in new business and enjoyed a flamboyant lifestyle that he shared with his several female companions. He liked motor cars to match, those including a Ford Zodiac convertible and a Mark II Jaguar (á la Morse). Fred stayed on wheeling and dealing for both Haiste and himself until the 1970s, but died young.

Highlights of the social calendar included cricket matches with Naylor Brothers and Ames Crosta. Haiste generally fielded the weaker team and contrived to bat first so that the opposition soon overhauled their meagre score and the pub session could get started sooner.

The turbulent 1970s

In 1970, JHH and the smaller firm of Arnold Brooksbank and Sons merged. Hugh Brooksbank became a partner of JHH and brought with him Michael Dyson, Alan McDonald, Phil Morris, Jim Prescott, Peter Roydhouse, Mike Tuson and Tony Withey.

Mr Sadler (Alf) was Brooksbanks 'elder statesman' and needed the odd cat nap to keep him going – he perfected the skill of nodding off with head propped up by hand and elbow on the desk, pencil positioned on paper in the other hand, as if deep in thought. But in his waking hours Alf was a great source of knowledge on all matters trade waste.

Peter Roydhouse, a 'gentle giant', owned and restored old motor cycles. When later working with me in Baghdad, I recall him pulling from his pocket a well thumbed manual on a Norton or similar machine, as light reading material in quiet moments or to keep himself engaged in useful endeavour during long meetings that weren't going anywhere.

The firm being in an expansionary phase, a number of associate partner appointments were also made at that time – Ian Aldred, Michael Dyson (from Brooksbanks), Graham Matthews, Derek Williams (successor to Ken Barker at M&E) and Tony Venn (head of structural department). They were followed in the mid 70s by Ian Crutchley, who established a presence for Haiste in the north west of England, initially in Liverpool then in Wrexham.

In 1974, a cataclysmic event occurred that spelled the death knell for many small-medium sized consultants working on public sector infrastructure projects, namely a massive reorganisation of local government. Overnight, Haiste effectively lost all of its public sector clients, the old UDCs and RDCs being swept away and larger authorities being consolidated into the new framework of metropolitan, county and district councils, together with the formation of the regional water authorities.

All of these new and larger authorities had assembled technical departments that sought to handle much of the routine work that was the bread and butter of Haiste and similar consultants. At the same time they were wrestling with their forward budgets and scheme priorities, the combined result being a rapid drying up of new local and water authority commissions. As a consequence, staff had to be made redundant for the first time in the firm's history and Section Leaders had the unenviable task of deciding who was to be given the word and then informing them.

Tough times, but fortunately the partners had started to explore and successfully exploit the overseas market with activity of very considerable commercial and technical challenge, notably in Iran, Iraq, Italy, Libya, Nigeria and Spain in the first instance. On the back of these projects, some being hugely profitable but others resulting in substantial losses, the firm did survive, but the financial consequences subsequently led to a radical change in ownership and structure.

At around this time a new event on the social calendar was the 'Haiste Olympics', held in the grounds of Belmont House. No photographic record of these exhibitions of skill and daring seem to be available, perhaps for good reason, but I recall very clearly that a small but deceptively powerful cleaning lady was unbeatable in the welly-wanging.

1980s, the last Haiste decade

In about 1981 Haiste became one of the first consulting firms to be incorporated and have limited liability status, with external shareholding as well as equity held by the partners who had now become company directors. It was a daring move at the time and was thought by the consulting engineering establishment to be somehow unprofessional and overly commercial. Haiste partners were obliged to resign their membership of the Association of Consulting Engineers. But these same establishment figures found themselves following exactly the same route in the years to follow and so the rules of the club were changed to suit.

The name John H Haiste and Partners had been simplified to Haiste and Partners in the late 1970s and it changed again to Haiste International Ltd. when the partnership was dissolved and the limited liability company was formed. At this time more than 80% of fee income was being generated from overseas, being reflected in the choice of company name. In 1982, Haiste's achievement was recognised by a Queens Award for Export.

As the 1980s progressed, the home market recovered in fits and starts and some big money earners overseas, such as Baghdad sewerage and the Libyan textile factories and solid waste projects, wound down. But the international department kept up their marketing efforts and secured prestigious projects in Athens and Tunis.

In about 1984, the firm went through another and very major restructuring with the creation of a holding company, Haiste Group Ltd, under the chairmanship of David Ball. Operating companies Haiste Ltd, Haiste Automation Ltd, Haiste M & E Ltd, Haiste Structures Ltd, Haiste International Ltd. and Haiste Services Ltd. were formed and a regional structure was overlaid. A thrust into the Scottish market was also realised through the purchase of a small M & E practice which was re-badged as Haiste Strain and Robertson.

By this stage the directors had achieved their aim of diversification and the concept of cost centres, both by discipline and by office / region, and tight financial project control had become established, years ahead of some of the big name consultants. Under David Ball's watchful eye, and with Geoff Bowyer recruited from Anglian Water as managing director, David Keegan, the financial director, pushed this forward relentlessly in his own inimitable style. The system meant that, financially, there was no place to hide, as Steve Day reminds me.

The company had come a long way and although it was now operating under modern management methods that are now commonplace, financially it was surviving rather than prospering, struggling to make consistent profits for its shareholders. Thus it was that in 1988, Carl Bro, a successful and cash rich Danish consulting firm operating in benign home and overseas markets and wanting to expand by acquisition, saw in Haiste exactly what they were looking for – a company that had an operating and management model that wouldn't have to be overhauled radically to bring it into line with Carl Bro principles, access to the UK market and strengthening of their international division by virtue of the high standing of British consultants in the international sphere.

Inevitably, Carl Bro's acquisition was not without its problems, including the new owner's decision to acquire a medium sized Scottish consultant soon after procuring Haiste. The integration of Haiste's small Scottish office with its much larger partner was especially troublesome, becoming one of the battlegrounds for the merger of the two UK firms, this process occupying a great deal of management time and taking years to resolve.

The Haiste name survived, as Carl Bro Haiste, for a few years longer into the early 90s and the rest as they say is (modern) history.

Domestic Footnote:

Nurturing at Haiste provided a sound grounding for a number of Haiste employees to leave the fold and establish enterprises of their own: Brian Smith (joined by Mike Jones) – Hydraulic Analysis; Bob Adcock and Ian Aldred – AA Associates; Arthur Burgess – Brentwood Engineering; Paul Hutchinson and Ian Whitlam – Hutchinson Whitlam Associates; David Calam and Graham Stevenson – Stevenson Calam Associates; Jim Gabbitas and Barry Gill – GGP Consult.

International Footnote:

In the 1970s and 80s we updated our international prospectus many times, but invariably it would open with the line that Haiste had been active internationally since the firm's beginnings in the 1920s, the Nyali Bridge in Kenya being quoted in this regard. A grainy black and white photograph of the bridge existed, but the circumstances of how JHH became involved with it we never knew.

A small boy named Manu Kukadia lived beside the creek that the bridge crossed. Manu was fascinated by this 'wobbly' (pontoon) bridge and grew up to become a civil engineer and bridge designer himself. In 2004 he joined Carl Bro in Leeds and discovered this link with his past. In 2010 Manu learned about the reunion and I had no hesitation in granting his request to join us.

Hugh Allan

In the Proximity of Evil

In Iraq

Acts of cruelty committed by one human being against another come in a seemingly infinite variety of truly dreadful forms. The most recent spate of evil barbarism of a widespread nature, claimed by its misguided adherents to be enacted in the name of their deity, has afflicted a part of the world with which I have some familiarity and empathy, and has spilled over into Europe in random acts of senseless and indiscriminate murder in our cities.

In 2014, the city of Ramadi in Iraq, the location of my first overseas assignment, was over-run and captured by 'Daesh' or 'so-called Islamic State' in Iraq and Syria (ISIS). It was freed two years later by Iraqi state troops with support from Iranian supported militia, both events causing much loss of life and human misery as people fled from their homes in fear and desperation. Further to the north, the city of Samarra, where we had a water supply project in the late 1970s, was also over-run by followers of that cult, which imposes on the cruelly suppressed population a way of living that is contrary to all concepts of what it should mean to be human, the very antithesis of the civilisation that was once cradled in those lands.

When I visited the town of Samarra it was a peaceful place, pleasantly situated on a hill above the River Tigris (the source of raw water for our water supply scheme), overlooking a fine barrage built in the 1950s to the design of British consulting engineers Coode and Partners. We walked about freely, mingling with its residents in the streets and markets. We joined them as visitors to a most impressive artefact from the ninth century, the 52m high spiral minaret that, more than a thousand years later, was still in sound condition, the stone pathway that leads to the top being worn but passable.

Men, women and children were enjoying a day out, foreign visitors were welcomed to join them on climbing the tower. They had no fear and reached the top. As I was going up women and children were coming down, generally holding on to the handrail that was fitted to the inside. Finding myself close to the outside of the path that lacked a handrail on that side I chickened out after the second level. If there was a pent up desire for a harsher and less humane manner of existence, it wasn't apparent to me then.

The largest non domestic consumer of water in Samarra that we had to allow for in our designs was a pharmaceutical factory. In the 1980s, western intelligence sources believed that this facility was involved in producing chemical weapons that were used against Iranian forces in the Iraq-Iran war.

Saddam Hussein's regime was characterised by ruthless suppression of dissent in any form, torture and summary executions in the feared Abu Ghraib prison being commonplace. In another inhumane act he deployed chemical weapons against the people of the Kurdish town of Halabja, where men women and children died, indiscriminately, in horrific manner. Had these dreadful contrivances originated from Samarra where we had provided the water supply? Sadly Saddam was just the latest in a long line of caliphs and invaders who, over the centuries in that territory, enforced their rule with use of beheadings, mass slaughter of innocents, and public displays of mutilated bodies and parts thereof.

Collective punishment on an ethnic basis was also in Sadaam's repulsive repertoire – Sunni against Shia and Kurd. After crushing a Shia revolt in the cities, he turned his attention to the marsh Arabs of southern Iraq, draining the marshlands in an area lying to the east of one of 'our' four cities, Samawah, destroying their villages and their unique way of life and causing massive ecological damage.

In the UK

Closer to home there were two dark episodes that remain in my memory, separated by two decades but similar in their brutality.

A year or two older than me, Isabelle Cook lived in Mount Vernon, a residential neighbourhood adjacent to Garrowhill. I often saw Isabelle on the bus to and from school and I knew her to say hello to. At the Garrowhill and Mount Vernon end of the journey, the shortest routes took us along tracks and quiet paths through wooded and undeveloped areas. On one of those journeys in December 1957, Isabelle was assaulted and murdered, not far from her home. There was a sombre mood at the school when her body was found and identified. The rector (headmaster) made an announcement at morning assembly and prayers were said.

The perpetrator was the infamous serial killer, Peter Manuel. Isabelle was his last victim and when caught by the police he confessed to her murder. He agreed to take officers to the place where he had buried her body. Arriving at the location, he was asked if he could pinpoint the grave, to which he is reported to have replied coldly: "I'm standing on her now"[19]. Manuel was convicted of seven murders and was executed by hanging on the 11th of July 1958, at Barlinnie Prison in Glasgow.

My young sister, Jo, attended Uddingston Grammar School and made a similar daily journey. Many years later, after my father's death, she told me that on one occasion she had been followed and had had to run home, she was convinced it had been Peter Manuel. I asked her why she didn't say anything at the time, but she replied that no one would have believed her.

Like Manuel before him, Peter Sutcliffe, the so-called "Yorkshire Ripper", was a serial killer. His final victim was Jacqueline Hill, whose body was found in 1980 on the grounds of the Lupton students' residences of the University of Leeds, behind the Arndale Centre in Headingley and a short walk from our office.

The police were distracted by taped messages sent to them by a person claiming to be the killer – "Wearside Jack". Led by Inspector George Oldfield, the police gave credence to the tape and the population was scoured in search of men who they thought fitted the profile. One of those interviewed was a colleague of mine at Haiste. From Tyneside rather than Wearside he was otherwise a match, and crucially he worked a few hundred yards from where Miss Hill's body was found. He was eliminated from their enquiries, but for me it brought back memories of poor Isabelle.

Notes and Bibligraphy

1 Moore, J. 1981. Taming Ancient Rivers of Greece. London: Faraway Books.

2 Barton, R. K. 2012. Waiting for the Rains. Pudsey, Leeds: Dovetail Press.

3 The Peter Principle is a concept in management developed by Laurence J. Peter, which observes that people in a hierarchy tend to rise to their level of incompetence.

4 Wilson R. Old Baillieston, Garrowhill and Easterhouse. Ochiltree, Ayrshire: Stenlake Publishing.

5 kester1940. 2010. The Clyde Valley Stompers – Peter and the Wolf. [Online]. [Accessed September 2018]. Available from https://www.youtube.com/watch?v=s9k1VRuil4Q

6 Uddingston. A small town of only 5000 population but the birthplace of some notable figures: James W Black, a doctor and pharmacologist who received the Nobel Prize in 1988; Jimmy Johnstone, footballer who made 515 appearances for Glasgow Celtic including playing in the first British team to take the European Cup, defeating Inter Milan in the 1967 final; Thomas Tunnock, who founded the bakery dynasty which in 1952 presented the world with the Tunnock's Caramel Wafer. Wikipedia. 2018. [Online]. [Accessed September 2018] Available from: https://en.wikipedia.org/wiki/Uddingston.

7 Darren Girvan. 2015. *Demolition of Red Road Flats* [online]. [Accessed October 2018] Available from: https://www.youtube.com/watch?v=pAV12_sf93M

8 Planimeter. A desk top device for measuring the area of an irregular shape.

9 Inflation Calculators. 2018. [Online]. [Accessed September 2018]. Available from: www.inflationdata.com.

10 Roberts G., Fowler D. 1995. Built by Oil. Reading: Ithaca Press.

11 Marozzi J. 2014. Baghdad, City of Peace, City of Blood. London: Allen Lane, Penguin Books.

12 Commonwealth War Graves Commission, Kut War Cemetery. 2018. [Online]. [Accessed September 2018]. Available from: https://www.cwgc.org/find-acemetery/cemetery/69700/KUT%20 WAR%20CEMETERY.

13 Allan H. A. 1984. Structural Design of Buried Rigid Pipelines, A Comparative Study of International Practice. In: Planning, Construction, Maintenance and Operation of Sewerage Systems 12-14 September 1984, Reading. BHRA, The Fluid Engineering Centre, Cranfield, Bedford. Paper G1, page 279.

14 Allan H. A. 1980. Specifying and Designing Buried GRP Gravity Pipelines. In: PIPECON80. London 1980. Paper 6-1.

15 From eulogy given by his son at E. A Drew's funeral service in February 2015.

16 Screech owl – a small nocturnal woodland owl found in the Americas.

17 "Unaccounted for Water" was a term in common use at the time, a catch-all for the sum total of losses. Later superseded by the term Non Revenue Water.

18 Gordon P., Doughan D. 2001. Dictionary of British Women's Organisations, 1825-1960. London: Woburn Press.

19 Naughton, N. 2014. Glasgow's East End. London: Transworld Publishers.